# RELIEF CARVING
# WOOD SPIRITS

by Lora S. Irish

FOX CHAPEL
PUBLISHING

Interior photos by Lora S. Irish

ISBN 978–1–56523–333–1

Irish, Lora S.

      Relief carving wood spirits / by Lora S. Irish. -- East Petersburg, PA:
Fox Chapel Publishing, c2008.
          p. ; cm.
          ISBN: 978-1-56523-333-1
          1.Wood-carving--Technique. 2.Relief (Decorativearts)
      3. Green Man (Tale) in art. 4. Spirits in art. I. Title.

TT199.7 .I758 2008
731.54--dc22                        0806

To learn more about the other great books from
Fox Chapel Publishing, or to find a retailer near you,
call toll-free 800-457-9112 or visit us at *www.FoxChapelPublishing.com*.

**Note to Authors:** We are always looking for talented
authors to write new books in our area of woodworking, design,
and related crafts. Please send a brief letter describing your idea to
Acquisition Editor, 1970 Broad Street, East Petersburg, PA 17520.

Printed in China
First printing: June 2008
Second printing: March 2010

## Dedication

To all the members of the *Woodcarving Illustrated* message board. Their open sharing of ideas, techniques, and experiences has encouraged so many new and advanced carvers to expand their work to new horizons.

## Acknowledgments

My special thanks go to Bob Duncan, *Woodcarving Illustrated* magazine editor and the moderator of the message board. Bob worked right alongside me throughout the creation of the original tutorial that is posted to the message board. His encouragement, great suggestions, and questions added depth and definition to the project.

# A Note from the Author

As a member of *Woodcarving Illustrated* magazine's message board, I enjoy the opportunity to share my work, experiences, and techniques with a worldwide group of woodcarvers and woodburners. The membership of the forum is made up of a variety of carvers, including character, bird, and animal carvers who work in three dimensions, relief carvers who work in two dimensions, and pyrographers who work in a single dimension. All are willing to add their ideas, suggestions, and inspiration to any thread or posting.

During one of our discussions on the board, a new member and new woodcarver asked if there were any tutorials or lesson plans that included all of the steps and all of the photos a carver used to create a work. As an author, I know including that many steps can be a problem because there simply is not enough space in a magazine article—or even an instruction book—to show each and every time a carver changes his tool or makes a cut with his knife.

The digital format of WCI's message board seemed a perfect place for me to try a complete tutorial. I began posting the Grape Man Wood Spirit carving tutorial on June 26, 2006, and it finished with more than 250 steps, more than 300 photos, and lots of fun chat back and forth from the message board members.

When the Grape Man Wood Spirit was completed, Fox Chapel Publishing, the parent company of WCI, graciously approached me about converting this tutorial into a workbook format. The editors wanted to make this step-by-step lesson plan available to any carver, whether new or well seasoned.

This tutorial was created with the idea of showing, in print, each and every step that goes into a carving. My goal is to show you everything—every cut, every tool change, and every depth check. As we work together, I will also share why each tool is used, why some areas are worked with a different approach, and what thinking goes into the planning of a carving project. We will explore the relationships of each area of the face, basic carving cuts, why some cuts are used for a particular area of work, and which tools work best for those cuts.

Although the step-by-step may seem massive and complicated, it's not. It is a simple beginner's project, taught as if you were sitting next to me at my carving table.

***Woodcarving Illustrated* Home Page**
http://www.woodcarvingillustrated.com/index.php

***Woodcarving Illustrated* Message Board**
http://www.woodcarvingillustrated.com/forum/index.php

## How to Use This Book

I have divided this book into three parts. The first part includes some general information on relief carving and wood spirits, the tools and materials you will need, and some techniques and skills you will learn.

The second part is the complete step-by-step process for creating the Grape Man Wood Spirit. It is broken down into the stages of relief carving and further broken down into smaller steps. Please read each section of work before you start any step for that section. Working in this manner will help you build an understanding of how individual cuts and strokes become one small part of an overall carving technique. Also included in the demonstration are tips for help along the way and The Larger Picture sections that show you the main goals for the section.

The third and final part features additional patterns made specifically for the carving lessons and new skills you have acquired. At the end of this book, you will have learned many of the basic and advanced techniques used to create relief woodcarving, no matter what the theme or subject of the pattern. I hope your newfound skills will inspire you to try other relief carvings in whatever subjects strike you.

—Lora S. Irish

# Contents

# Part 1

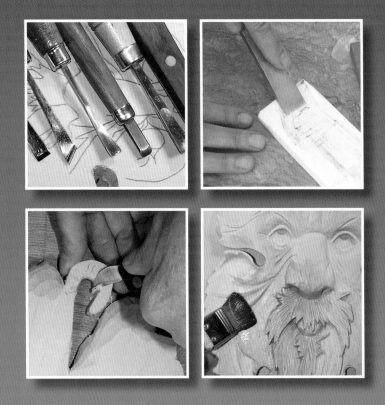

# Getting Started in Relief Carving

Before you undertake any actual carving, you'll need to lay the groundwork for success. In this section, we'll look at the relief carving process, the tools and materials you'll need, and some useful skills and techniques so you're well prepared when you make your first cut.

# About Relief Carving and Wood Spirits

One way to prepare yourself to carve is to learn as much as you can about the carving style you're using and the subject you plan to carve. Here, we'll take a look at what relief carving is, what the carving process is, and how wood spirits fit into that style of carving.

## What Is Relief Carving?

Relief carving is a style of woodcarving in which all of the dimensional work is done to the face of the wood and the back of the wood is left mostly unworked or smooth, compared to three-dimensional carvings where every side of the wood is worked. There are two main types of relief carving: low relief and high relief. Each type differs in how the joint lines between elements are carved. We will be working with techniques from both types of relief carving as we create the Grape Man Wood Spirit.

### Low Relief Carving

Low relief carving is done in definable layers, yet the entire carved surface has a shallow look to it. Low relief does not necessarily mean that the wood surface is carved to a very small depth; it

From *Wildlife Carving in Relief*, Lora S. Irish, Fox Chapel Publishing, Inc., 2000.

*Buffalo Portrait* is carved in the low relief style. The pattern has been worked using levels and layers to give a stepped effect to the design. Worked on a ¾" basswood board, the carving reaches ½" into the wood along the joint between the background and portrait. It has been finished with Danish oil. Note the color tones the Danish oil gives to the heart wood grain that runs through the center of the bread board.

An example of low relief carving, *Springhouse Barn* uses very simple rounded-over edges between areas. Note the reflection created in the pond directly below the springhouse lean-to addition on the barn. The piece is carved in ½" Honduras Mahogany and finished with Danish oil.

*Note: The patterns used to create the four projects here can be found in the books noted in the credit lines.*

From *Landscapes in Relief: Carving Techniques and Patterns*, Lora S. Irish, Fox Chapel Publishing, Inc., 2000.

instead refers to the visual impression that the carving creates because all the intersecting joint lines are visible. The edge of one carved area slants down to the next intersecting level, and the joint between the two areas can easily be seen. In the images on page 2, you can see that the carved edges meet where they can be seen and that no area casts a definite shadow onto the next to imply deep carving. By using the low relief technique, you anchor the pattern to the wood background through the visible intersections, which emphasize the impression that the design has been cut into the carving block.

Although this type of carving has a shallow effect, it's important to establish different levels within the work. Leaves of a floral design that are tucked under the flower's petals should appear to be lower in the work than the flower, yet should lie on top of the background. In addition, low relief often has an abundance of fine detail.

## High Relief Carving

In high relief carving, the joint lines, which are so obvious in low relief carving, are invisible. Undercuts are used to hide the intersections of individual areas of work by reaching underneath the upper element to make a trough between that element and the one below it. These undercuts, or troughs, create the impression of depth because one area appears to float above another and because the high area now casts a shadow on the surface below. Because of the shadows created through the undercuts, a high relief carving has a more dramatic depth effect than a low relief carving. An undercut does not need to be deep to create dramatic shadows. Only enough wood needs to be removed to create a shadowed effect in the carving.

From *Wildlife Carving in Relief*, Lora S. Irish, Fox Chapel Publishing, Inc., 2000

*Red Fox Resting* takes on a three-dimensional look by using the shadow box effect, through which deep undercuts are made and some of the elements in the design are freed from the background. The fox is worked on a ¾" basswood plaque.

From *Landscapes in Relief: Carving Techniques and Patterns*, Lora S. Irish, Fox Chapel Publishing, Inc., 2000

*Springhouse*, created in 4/4 Butternut with a Linseed Oil finish, uses deep undercutting with a bench knife to give dramatic effect to a high relief carving. The shadows created by the undercuts imply greater depth than the carving actually has. Butternut shows a strong-grained look throughout the work and a delightful silver tone when finished.

## Wood Spirits

Historically, relief carving has been a common and effective style for creating wood spirits. Often called or linked to Green Men, wood spirits are usually portrayed as male faces within the leaves. More than just carved ornaments, however, wood spirits were interpretations of myths and stories, designed to "place a face on nature," or make nature more understandable. Like most myths, the stories tried to explain natural occurrences that were not understood because of the very limited scientific or physiological knowledge of the time. Many stories used personification, giving an inanimate object human characteristics. These images appear in almost every culture, although their earliest documented appearance was in Rome.

In one of the early stories, Mother Nature, the Sun and creator of all life, wanted to come to earth and enjoy the beautiful world that she had created—to walk the fields and forests. However, she became lonely walking by herself. To ease her loneliness, her consort also came to earth by inhabiting the trees of both the meadows and the forests. He stood as the single old apple tree that graced the grasslands, giving shade to the cattle and goats, or as the guardian of the forest, the largest tree right at the forest margin. He was the oldest twisted tree deep within the black woods. Though in the heavens he was the Moon, on earth he was called the Spirit of the Woods.

It was believed that his favorite tree was the evergreen. Humans knew that the pines and conifers were special because even during the coldest and harshest of winters they remained forever green. Other trees suffered the "small death" of winter, losing their leaves and going bare. The story arose that Mother Nature's consort went into the evergreen to live during the winter and there he slept until the warmth of spring returned.

Because people were frightened that the "small death" might one day not give way to spring, they decided to go to the forest and bring evergreens into their homes. They would tend the evergreen, giving it water and protecting it from the deep snows and harsh winds. Therefore, they were protecting the Spirit of the Woods through the worst of the winter months. When the time came that the "small death" of winter should be passing, they would return the evergreen to its place within the forest so that the god would awaken and once again bring spring to the earth.

Although some of the stories faded as Christianity took hold, wood spirits continued to appear in a variety of places. They can still be found in cathedrals as ornaments carved in wood or stone. Relief-carved wood spirits were particularly popular because with their decorative leaves and other branching elements, they could easily be used to fill spaces, such as areas on walls and columns.

Even today, the wood spirit sometimes touches our daily lives. The tradition of the Christian Christmas tree that is brought into homes and brightly decorated each December is one such example. In carving, wood spirits have seen a revival, and modern three-dimensional carving styles are often employed to capture these images. I've chosen the older relief style for this book because it makes a great beginning relief project, keeping the focus on the face and learning the facial structures.

Wood spirits are often depicted as old men with windswept hair. (The pattern for this project is found on page 108.)

# The Process of Relief Carving

For those of you new to relief carving, it will be helpful if you understand the general process before you begin. In addition to the wood preparation and the finishing, relief carving has four distinct stages: roughing out, smoothing, detailing, and cleaning up. Each stage plays an important part in creating the finished piece.

**Preparing the wood:** As with most carving, several simple steps must precede ever picking up a carving tool, including tracing the pattern, sanding and smoothing the surface, and cutting the wood to shape.

Wood preparation includes planning, sizing the board, cutting the outline shape, sanding the surface, and tracing the pattern.

**Roughing out:** Roughing out begins with establishing the different levels and layers of carving depths by mapping out the pattern. Each area is roughly carved to a general depth in the wood, using techniques such as stop cuts and tools such as chisels and gouges. Roughing out can also be called "hogging out" or "leveling out." Once each area has been dropped to its particular depth in the wood blank, each element can be rounded or rolled over to give shape to that element. Shadows are created using either a low relief visible joint line or a high relief undercut.

## Micro tools

My tool kit contains three micro tools. These are very small, thin-faced tools, perfect for extremely tight work. The first is the ⅛" U-gouge, sometimes called a veiner, which is perfect for teasing out wood in very tight, deep angles. The second is a micro straight chisel. The cutting edge of this chisel is only ⅛" wide, which makes it perfect for working very tight or confined spaces. My third micro tool is a miniature dogleg chisel. This particular tool is only ½" long in the dogleg area and has a ⅛" profile cutting edge. As you increase the tools in your kit, you may wish to consider adding these three specialty micro tools.

## Depth Gauge

For relief carving, nothing measures as well as a depth gauge. This small ruler has a sliding "T" that can be set at the depth of the wood thickness to make sure that elements in the same level are carved to the correct depth. You can buy a commercial depth gauge or make your own. See Making a Depth Gauge on page 48 to make one for this project. You can use the same techniques for any project.

A compass and a straightedge or ruler are often used with a depth gauge. Compasses transfer depth measurements and straightedges are great for checking that elements are the same level.

A commercial depth gauge looks like a small ruler with a sliding T. Depth gauges, whether commercial or homemade, are indispensable for relief carving.

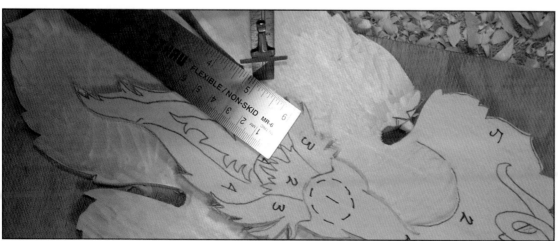

A straightedge, ruler, or any flat object helps to show depth from the uncarved areas of the wood.

# Wood

Listed here are some common woods for carving. Some, like butternut and basswood, are good choices for the beginner. As your skill level progresses, you can try some of the other woods that are a little more difficult to carve.

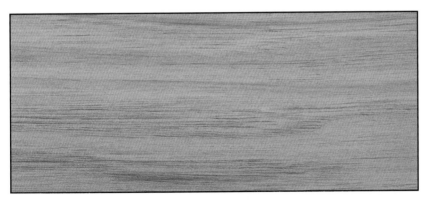

## Basswood (Tilia americana)

Also called American lime, basswood is a soft, creamy white wood that is easy to work and glues into larger blocks very well. I use basswood for many of my relief carving projects and chose it for this project because several of its features make it excellent for learning new techniques. Basswood has no figuring and has an extremely fine, straight, even grain that does not disturb or distort your carving cuts. It carves well, is lightweight, and is excellent for detail work. Because it is a soft wood, you won't need a lot of pressure to make cuts. These properties make basswood great for beginning carvers.

Basswood has one major drawback: It can require quite a bit of sanding and clean-up work. Because it is a soft-fibered and tight-fibered wood, it seems no matter how hard you work, there will always be a few "fuzz bunnies" left.

## Butternut (Juglans cinerea)

Butternut, also called white walnut, is much lighter in weight than black walnut, has a medium-fine straight grain, and is golden brown to reddish brown at the sapwood. If you use an oil finish, the carving's surface takes on a light oak tone. Butternut is excellent for high relief carving with some fine detailing and is often used in furniture carving and veneering. It is a great hand tool wood.

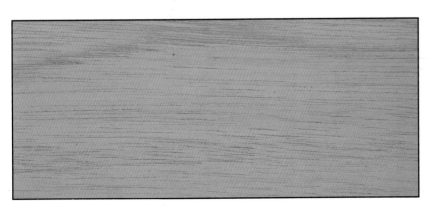

## Mahogany, Honduras (Swietenia macrophylla)

Mahogany has a reddish tone that deepens beautifully over the years. It is a strong, yet light, wood with a straight and even grain. It shaves well and takes extremely fine detail. Mahogany can be carved using hand tools, mallet tools, or power tools.

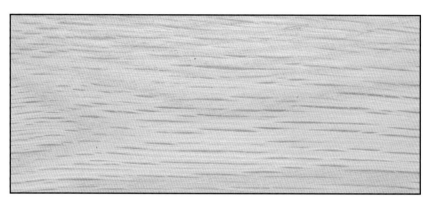

### White Oak (Quercus alba)

Oak is a hard wood with strong grain lines that has long been a favorite of woodcarvers. It is often used in furniture making, where it can be deeply carved to create sculptured legs, drawer fronts, and headboards. The light golden tones of the wood mature into a deep russet brown with time. White oak is often carved using mallet tools or power tools.

### Sugar Pine (Pinus lambertiana)

The dramatic grain of pine can sometimes create problems for the woodcarver because it can distort the smoothing and detailing steps of your work. Sugar pine is the exception to the species because it has less dramatic tight grain and carves like butternut or mahogany. The clear, white color of the pine becomes a golden orange patina with time. Sugar pine is easily carved using hand tools.

### Black Walnut (Juglans nigra)

The density and deep brown tones of black walnut make it an excellent carving wood. Walnut has tight, dark black grain lines that add to the rich coloring of the wood. Mallet tools and power tools are often chosen for carving walnut.

## Preparation Tools

In addition to the tools you'll need for the actual carving process, there are other tools that will make the job of preparing for carving easier. You certainly don't need to purchase all of them; simply choose the ones you need or find most useful.

A bench hook supports the carving and holds it in place as you work, and a terry cloth towel catches chips for easy cleanup.

### Working Surfaces and Safety Items

One of the first things you'll want to do for relief carving is set up your workspace. I suggest a bench hook or bracing board to support the relief carving during the early stages of carving. Later, when you're doing more delicate work, you can use router pads or nonskid pads beneath the wood. These pads are about ¼" thick and grab both the work surface (your table) and the carving. Router pads can be purchased at most hardware stores. Nonskid foam pads, the kind you find for lining your kitchen cabinets, or soft foam pads that come in shipping boxes also hold the wood and compensate for any rocking motion. Even something as simple as several sheets of paper towels can be folded and stuffed under an area of a relief carving to prevent rocking. Keep an eye out for small padded items that can be added to your kit.

A thick terry cloth towel is a staple in my carving kit. I fold the towel into quarters and lay it over my lap to support the wood when I cannot work the carving on the bench hook. I place my holding hand under the towel to protect that hand from any possible cuts. Terry cloth also grabs wood chips, making cleanup much easier. When the carving is in a bench hook, I place the terry cloth towel on the table first, and then situate the bench hook over the towel to protect my worktable.

Leather aprons are also great when you are carving in your lap instead of at a worktable. The leather protects your legs from possible cuts and catches chips for easy cleanup. Scrap-leather lap blankets can be inexpensively made by cutting out the back section from an old leather coat.

A carving glove is important if the hand that's not holding the tool is holding the wood or is near the cutting action. You may also want a thumb guard for the hand holding the tool if you perform a lot of paring cuts, where the knife comes toward your thumb.

Use a nonskid pad between the carving and the bench hook to keep the relief carving from rocking.

### Tip

Though I use some specialized tools, it is not necessary to have all of them in your kit. Many times your favorite tool can be used in place of what you see being used in an article or a book. This is a simple carving, so use the tools you already have. As you work, you will discover which tool gives you the best results.

## Dusting Tools

Never throw away an old *toothbrush*. Instead, put it right into your tool kit. Toothbrushes are great for getting dust out of the undercuts.

An *ox-hair oil paintbrush* works well but is a more expensive dusting tool. Some ox-hair brushes have very long bristles that can reach into the deepest areas of your carving.

*Compressed air*, either from an air compressor or from a can, can quickly blow loose chips or dust from the surface of your carving.

Keep brushes on hand to sweep dust from the crevices of your carving.

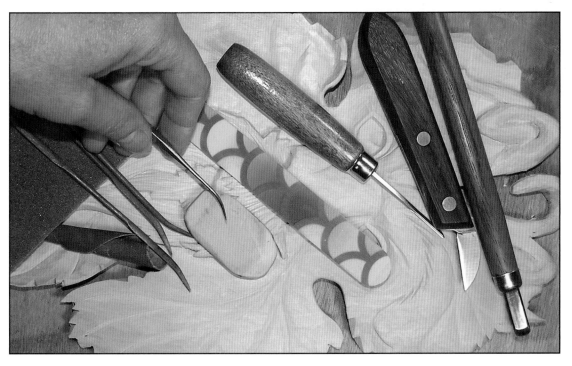

Fingernail files, dental picks, and white artist erasers all aid you in cleaning up your carving and preparing it for finishing.

# Sharpening and Honing Tools

Sharpening and honing your tools are essential parts of carving, but they can also be very complicated topics to address. You'll want to pick up a book or a DVD that focuses on the techniques of tool sharpening. In the meantime, here are a few pointers on tools to help you keep the edges of your tools in fine cutting order.

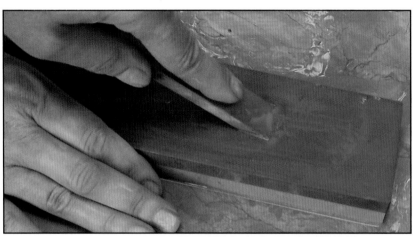

I am giving a large, flat chisel a quick sharpening on an 800-grit Japanese water stone. Notice that the entire face of the tool is against the stone, and I rub the tool back and forth in a long stroke. Whenever you pull or push, try not to lift the tool at the end of each stroke.

## Sharpening Stones

Sharpening stones are categorized by their material makeup, the grit size, and what type of lubricant is used. You'll want to have two sharpening stones: one that is *coarse*, about 800 grit, and one that is *fine*, about 8,000 grit. It doesn't matter what type of stone you use; they can be water stones, oilstones, diamond stones, or ceramic stones, to name a few. Just make sure that you follow the instructions for whatever stone you use. Some stones, for example, can be used wet or dry, while other stones must have a lubricant.

If the tool is very dull or improperly shaped, start with the coarse stone. Then, move to the fine stone to remove the abrasions from the coarse stone and to hone the edge. Once you're happy with the edge, you'll want to strop the tool, as discussed in the next section. After the face is profiled and angled on the coarse stone, you should not need to return to the coarse stone during any carving session unless you have damaged or dented the tool's edge. Returning too often to the coarse stone is a common beginner's error because a coarse stone destroys all of the sharpening work that followed it. Remember, use the coarse stone to establish the face and angle; then, use the finer stone to refine the cutting edge. Any freshening of the edge should be done either with your finest stones or strops.

This is the finer, 6,000-grit Japanese water stone. I spend about 15 minutes working with this second stone.

If I need to reestablish an edge or touch up just one tool, I often go directly to ceramic stones. This set, one brown 800 grit and one white 8,000 grit, are palm size and perfect for storage in my carving kit for quick use.

## Check Your Tools Often

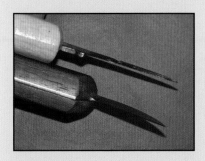 

In these photos, there are two knives. The top one is a very old bench knife that is not made of good steel and has never held an edge. I don't know why I have kept it all these years except that it is a good example of a poorly sharpened tool. Notice all the shiny spots along the edge of the bench knife. Every one of them is a ding or a dull spot on the cutting edge. Because those areas of the edge are not absolutely sharp, the dull or flattened area can reflect light. This light test is a fast way to check a tool that is causing you problems. Put the tool under a light and if you can see the edge or see highlights, the tool is dull.

Now look at the chip carving knife just below the bench knife. It has no spots and no highlights. In fact, it is so sharp you cannot see the actual edge. All of your tools should look like this.

Finish all sharpening sessions with a newspaper honing. The fine texture of the paper gives your knife that extra polish, and the ink acts as your honing compound.

## Strops

If your tools are in relatively good shape but are a little dull, all you'll need to do is strop, or hone, the tool to create the final polish. I like to use a *leather strop* and *honing compound* or *roughing compound*. Leather strops come with one side of tanned leather and a second side of raw leather. Work the raw side first and then add a final polish using the tanned side. Synthetic strops are also available and are well worth the investment because they have an extremely smooth and even consistency to their surface.

Strop both sides of your tool's edge equally and strop often. I check the edges of my tools frequently during a session and probably strop a tool about every 20 to 30 minutes of work. I use a fair amount of downward pressure during the stropping session and strop for about 5 to 10 minutes. Constant stropping keeps the tool's edge pristine and sharp and does a great deal to avoid needing to redo or retouch cutting edges.

Though a tool can be pushed back and forth on a stone, use only the pull stroke when stropping. By the time you strop, the tool's edge is sharp enough to cut into the leather if you use a push stroke.

I like to finish my stropping sessions with a newspaper honing. The fine texture of the paper gives your knife extra polish and the ink acts as honing compound. It's a good practice to sharpen your tools after each carving session so you can begin the next session with nicely sharpened edges.

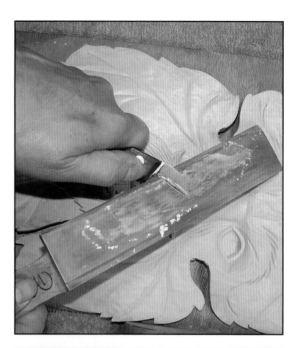

This is a synthetic strop with aluminum oxide powder. I also use a leather strop and red oxide rouge. Keep the tool very low on the strap for a tight-angled tool edge. Honing is a back-and-forth, pull-flip-pull motion that brings a tool's edge back to a sharp polish. Do it just like the barbers in the old Western movies when they were stropping a razor on a long leather belt.

# Finishes For Your Carving

There are a variety of finishes that you can use, and your choice should depend on what you want the finish to do, whether it's protect the carving or add color. We'll be using boiled linseed oil for the demonstration, but try some of the other finishes listed here as your carving experience increases.

## Finishes

*Boiled linseed oil* is a popular choice for finishing wood spirits because it brings out all the details, tucks, and rolls of the carving. This finish also yellows the wood over time. Consider that yellowing effect if you are adding color or paints to your wood. The oil will, over time, change the look of the paint color. For an unpainted carving, the yellowing effect can add character.

An advantage to boiled linseed oil finish for the beginning carver is that the carving can be reworked, or additionally carved, after the finish has been applied. Once the changes are made, a new, fresh coat of oil can be added and will completely blend into the earlier coatings.

*Danish oil* gives a wonderful finished effect, is extremely simple in its use, and stands up very well to handling. It does, however, tone the basswood to a golden color and can slightly change the look of any stains or acrylic paints that you may have used on the project.

*Paste wax* is the clearest of any of the final finishes. The very white color of basswood stays true, and stains are completely unchanged. However, paste wax does not hold up well to lots and lots of handling, so unless I am willing to occasionally reapply the wax, I use this finish only on the more decorative carvings. Even with its lack of long-term durability under constant handling, I admit I use it often just because carvings finished with paste wax feel excellent to hold.

*Polyurethane* and *urethane* are the most durable finishes for any carving that will receive a lot of use over its lifetime. I personally prefer the spray type of urethanes because of their convenience and ease to use. Polyurethanes do not distort the color of the wood, paints, or patina created from age, leaving only a clear, smooth finish.

*Paint*, both *acrylic* and *oil*, is a great way to add color to your carvings, and it can be used in addition to some of the finishes mentioned in this section. Both types of paints can be used at full strength, so the wood grain doesn't show through, or diluted, so the wood grain does show through.

Boiled linseed oil is a popular finish that bring out all of the details in a carving.

### Tools for Application

There are a number of useful accessories to keep on hand for finishing. *Lint-free cotton cloths* are most often used for wiping excess finish off the carving. They can sometimes be used for applying finish, too. Paper towels work well to protect your working surface.

A variety of *brushes* is extremely useful. I usually have a large ox-hair brush for applying the acrylics, a large soft brush for applying the oil paints, and small soft brushes in different shapes and sizes for general painting, getting into hard-to-reach areas, and dry brushing.

*Water pans*, *mixing pans*, and *paint palettes* aid you in thinning finishes and mixing paint. You'll also want to keep any *thinners*, such as turpentine, on hand for the finishes you use most often.

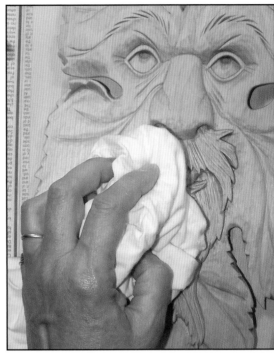

Use a lint-free cotton cloth to remove any excess oil.

A large soft brush works well for applying boiled linseed oil.

## Tip

Take care to dispose of oily rags properly because they can spontaneously combust. An easy way to take care of them is to soak them in a bucket of water. I soak the rags and newspaper, when I am completely done, in soapy water to break down the oil. Never throw the rags in a pile.

# Relief Carving Skills and Techniques

Because relief carving is its own subset of carving, you'll want to perfect the basic carving techniques and any special skills associated with relief carving. Let's look at the basic skills and techniques that we will be learning and using throughout this book. This section is organized by alphabetically order for easy reference as you work through your carving project.

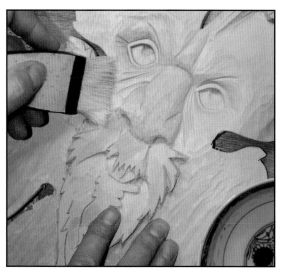

## Cleaning Up and Using Wet Checks

Relief carvers clean, tweak, and remove unwanted wood fibers throughout the carving process using an assortment of techniques, which can include making extra cuts, smoothing ridges, or sanding. A simple process called a wet check, in which you brush water on the carving, is used to determine how a carving will look when the oil finish has been applied and to raise or expose any loose wood fibers that need to be sanded down.

## Creating Shadows

Shadows are extremely important in relief carving because they give the carving added depth, and carvers use a variety of techniques to create different types of shadows.

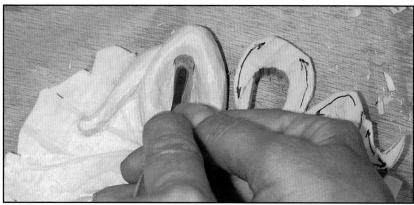

In this carving, we'll tuck stems and tendrils so they look like they curl under themselves, disappear in the curl, and re-emerge on the other side of the roll. This technique gives the illusion of continuity where one area of your carving disappears or tucks under another.

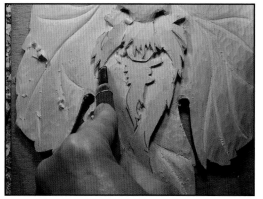

Undercutting the edges of the high elements creates an area of shadow on the lower elements in the carving. These shadows at depth and interest to your work.

### Shaping

Shaping is the relief carving term that refers to the rounding over and contour carving of any element. Round gouges, chisels and the bench knife are the tools used to shape an area. By shaping the edges and some of the back of the carving, carvers can create thick and thin shadows on the wall, adding to the impression of the leaf rolls and curves along the edge of the carving.

## ▲ Hogging Out

Carvers use this term to distinguish the times that they're removing a lot of wood at one time. In relief carving, hogging out is most often used in the early stage of creating levels for the elements in the design. This is the time to use larger tools, which will remove wood more quickly. Even though hogging out is meant to be reasonably quick with lots of progress, take care that you don't try to do too much at once and break or chip out any sections.

## ▼ Making a Stop Cut

The stop cut is a simple technique that physically separates one area from the next. Using this cut keeps you from carving off more than you intend to. For a simple stop cut, use a chip carving knife to make a thin, straight cut along the pattern line. To make a wide stop cut, cut straight into the wood along the pattern lines of the areas you wish to separate. Then, angle the knife so the tip of the knife cuts in to the depth of the first cut. When you finish, a V-shaped chip should pop out. Once the stop cut is complete, check to see if it allows you enough working room. If not, widen the cut by making a new knife cut in the same position as the original straight cut. Next, drop your knife to an angle wider than or below the chip angle to remove another wood chip. You can widen a stop cut as many times as necessary to open the chip trough enough to create working room for your next cuts.

## ▼ Making a Chip Cut

A chip cut is an easy way to remove a perfect triangle-shaped chip from the wood. This technique involves three cuts. First, working along one side of the triangle, angle the knife toward the center of the V and make a cut. Then, cut the second side of the triangle, again angling the knife in toward the center of the V. Next, hold the knife low on the wood and slice into the other two cuts. The chip should pop out.

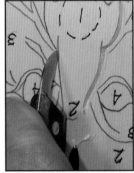

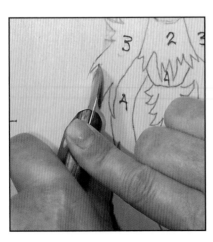
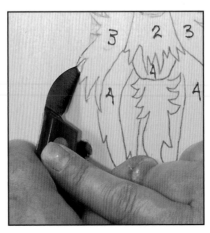

## ▼ Supporting Delicate Areas

Many relief carvings have areas that are delicate to cut because they are thin or because of the grain direction in that area. Support these delicate areas with your hand, a sanding pad, or an eraser during the carving process to prevent them from chipping out or breaking.

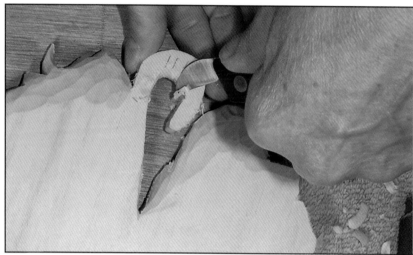

## ▲ Replicating the Human Face

The face on a wood spirit is strong, well-defined , and bold. It has deeply set eyes that lie below a high, wide brow ridge. The nose and nose bridge blend smoothly into the forehead area. The eye pupils and nostrils create the darkest shadows in the carving. Accurate placement of each of the facial features is essential to the pleasing look of the finished piece (see *Understanding Facial Anatomy* on page 30 for more details).

## ▼ Texturing

Texturing, also called detailing, adds character to carvings. In this carving, the serration of the leaf edges and the V-tool work in the mustache and beard are a dramatic change from the smooth curves and flow of the face. Small details like these will help bring your work to life.

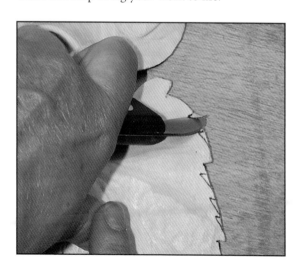

## ◄ Undercutting

Undercutting works a chip trough underneath the outer edge of an element, creating a shelf to that element's edge that casts shadows on the elements below it. Placing undercuts correctly is important to controlling the different types of shadows in relief carving. Undercuts are especially helpful for adding shadows inside the actual carving. The photo below helps explain the angles of the two cuts used to create an undercut area in a carving.

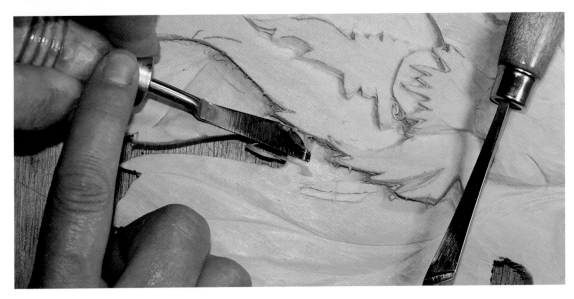

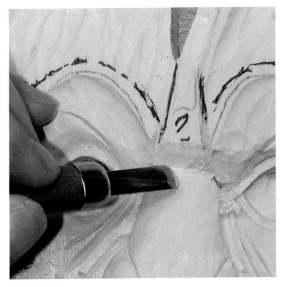

## ◄ Upending a Tool

Upending a tool makes the most of the profiles you have and can help you cut tight areas. By upending a round gouge, you can use the round profile to create half-circle stop cuts in your work. V-tools create V-shaped stop cuts. This technique can also help you make cleaner stop cuts than you can with a bench knife and can be used in a scraping motion to smooth out hard-to-reach areas. Using a tool on its profile does not damage the tool.

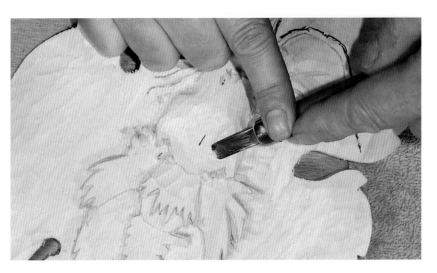

## ▲ Using a Tool Upside Down

Using a tool upside down provides you with more profiles for shaping specific parts. This technique also lets you shave thin slivers of wood with a tool that normally removes large amounts of wood.

## ▼ Walking the Band Saw

"Walking the band saw" means to make a cut, back up a little, and then make another cut right next to the first. This technique allows you to cut out thin slices and then continue making long cuts. Similar terminology is sometimes used with carving tools as well. To walk a tool to a cut is to approach a cut slowly, often in several passes.

# Understanding Facial Anatomy

When it comes to carving wood spirits, understanding basic facial anatomy is just as important as understanding how to cut wood with a gouge or a knife. Notice the depth in the *Twisted Beard Spirit* on page 31. This project is done on a 2" x 2" x 12" basswood block and has a fairly large face with definite facial planes. To get the same kind of depth in your project, use the following guidelines.

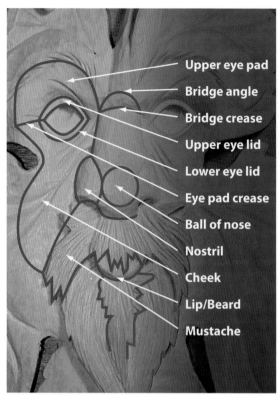

- Upper eye pad
- Bridge angle
- Bridge crease
- Upper eye lid
- Lower eye lid
- Eye pad crease
- Ball of nose
- Nostril
- Cheek
- Lip/Beard
- Mustache

This face map of the *Grape Man* shows parts that are common to wood spirit carvings. Identifying the same parts on each wood spirit you create can help you get the facial features just right.

- ❧ **Use your own face as a reference.** If you place your fingertip on the ball of your nose and let the bottom section of your finger touch your chin, you can feel that the nose ball, lips, and chin are all in line with each other, but they all taper away from the high point of the nose. In order of highest to lowest, it's the nose, upper lip, lower lip, and chin.
- ❧ **Make the lower lip deeper than the upper lip.** A high lower lip, one that is at the same level as or higher than the upper lip, makes the face look like it's pouting. When you go to paint a face, paint the lower lip a darker color because it is deeper than the upper one.
- ❧ **Notice that the brow ridge is lightly curved.** The outer edge of your eyebrows is lower on your face than the inner edge near the eye. Also notice that where the nose joins the brow ridge is above the top of the eye. One of the easiest carving mistakes is to make the eyes level with the top of the nose.
- ❧ **Carve the nose as a diamond, not a triangle.** The bottom section of the diamond is about one-third the size of the upper diamond area. Both parts of the diamond share the nostrils. The highest point of the nose is at the intersection of the two diamond halves, and the mouth falls down from the nose. Though the *Grape Man* only has a lower lip, he still has the downward curve where the mustache is marked in red. You can feel this curve along your face at the laugh lines, where the upper lip muscles join the cheek areas.
- ❧ **Know that everything on the face, except the nose, falls down from the point that the nose joins to the brow ridge.** As you age, those down lines become more dramatic with crow's feet around the eyes, and deep ridges under the eyes and falling down the cheeks.

- ❧ **Define the side view as two backward Z angles.** One zigzag is on the front of the face from the forehead to the brow, the brow to the nose joint, and down the nose. The second is from the corner of the eye, the deepest point of the face, forward down the cheek to the highest point in the cheek. From there, it goes back into the face to the lowest point of the cheek, and forward again along the bottom edge of the nostril.
- ❧ **Look at the features relative to each other.** Notice how low the nose tip is when compared to the rest of the face. The highest point of the brow, the nostrils, and the lips are all in the same line, or plane. The cheek's high point and the back of the nostril also fall on the same line. Remember, the eye is the deepest point of the face. The forehead falls away from the line starting at the brow ridge. A straight or falling-forward forehead distorts the nose. If you don't have an angled-back nose joining an angled-back forehead, your nose area will look funny. The hairline can be in the front of the face and go as far back into the face as the eyes.

In the *Twisted Beard Spirit* the red line shows where the original wood block surface was for reference.

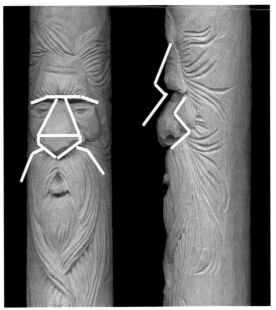

Notice how the nose is shaped like a diamond, not a triangle. Use two Z shapes to properly angle the side view.

On the *Apple Man*, the eyes are extremely high on the face. They are almost above the nose-brow joint, and that position makes the nose float, unattached to the carving. For this design, the eyes were raised to connect the face to the leaves that make up his brow ridge.

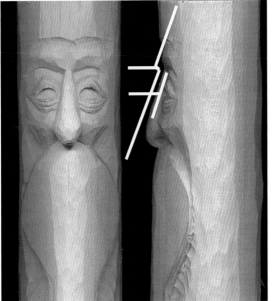

This photo shows an eye that has been placed too low compared to the joint of the nose and brow. Notice that the eye is almost halfway down the nose length. The forehead and nose slants are good, but the lower eyelid needs to be pushed way back into the face. Right now it is higher than the upper lid.

*Note: The two patterns used to create the two projects here can be found in* Wood Spirits and Green Men, *available from Fox Chapel Publishing.*

# Carving Eyes

In carving relief wood spirits, the eyes are the focus of the project. They are the first area of the carving that you notice, making it important to work them accurately. Though eyes are no harder than any other area of the face, new carvers often hesitate to attempt faces because of the eyes. Here is a small practice pattern to learn how to carve eyes in wood spirits.

For this sample, I am working with a 5" x 5" practice board square of basswood and a very simple wood spirit face. Follow the general steps on pages 38 and 39 to prepare the wood surface and trace the patterns. Then, carve through the eye carving steps.

As discussed in *Understanding Facial Anatomy* on page 30, the eyes and eyelids are set below the cheek and brow ridge. If you gently lay a ruler against your face over the center of the eye, the ruler will touch both of these areas but not the eye. Remember, the eyes are always the deepest area of the carving.

**Step 1:** Use the bull-nose chisel or straight chisel to drop the nose bridge area down to its level in the wood. This gives you a reference point for the depth of the eyes. The nose bridge is now about one-half the depth of the basswood. Just as with our Oak Man, I dropped the entire eye area below the nose bridge, about two-thirds of the basswood depth. Retrace the eye pattern and define the outer edges of the eye with a V-tool.

**Step 2:** Notice that the eye shape is not round or oval but almond shaped. The eyeball area in this early stage includes both eyelids. Once the eyeball area has been worked, draw a line along the upper third of the eyeball for the upper eyelid. The upper eyelid is wider and more dominant then the lower eyelid. With a V-tool, cut the upper eyelid line. Then, use a chisel to drop the eye area below that lid-line depth, which makes the top section of the eye lie below the upper eyelid.

**Step 3:** Mark the lower eyelid, and use the V-tool to carve along the line to define the lower lid. Just as with the upper eyelid, use the chisel to drop the lower section of the eye so it is below the lower eyelid. The lower lid is deeper than the upper lid. It is also thinner, usually about one-half the width of the upper lid.

**Step 5:** The eyeball lies inside the two eyelids and is deeper than the eyelids, so carve the eyeball down. Keep the eyeball slightly round so it tucks into the corners near the nose and along the temples. Because the piece is small, I used a fine U-gouge. This is probably the most important step because the eyelids must look as though they can close over the eyeball. The highest point of the eyeball must be lower than the edges of the upper and lower eyelids.

**Step 4:** With both eyelids V-tooled, the eyeball area is divided into three distinct sections. Notice that the lower eyelid is slightly shorter than the upper eyelid. The lower lid does not join the upper lid at the corner but just inside the outer point of the upper lid. By shortening this lid, you allow the inside edge of the lower lid to show and become part of the upper lid both on the inner and outer edges of the eyeball.

# Part 2

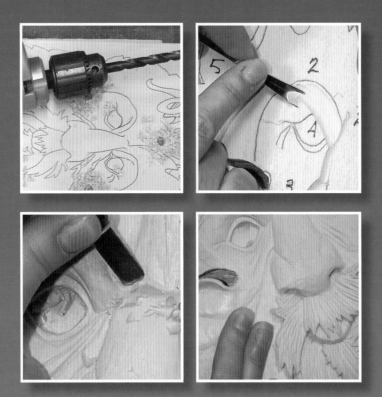

# Carving a Wood Spirit

Now that you've learned the basics of the process, the tools and materials, and some skills and techniques, you're ready to begin carving. You'll find a comprehensive tools and materials list along with the pattern on the following pages. Then, I'll take you through each stage of the carving process to complete our Grape Man Wood Spirit.

# What You'll Need

### Wood

Basswood blank, 9" wide x 14" long x ¾" or 1" thick

### Carving Tools

Bench knife

Chip carving knife

Small round gouge

Large round gouge

Wide-sweep gouge

¼" 45-degree V-tool

⅛" 45-degree V-tool

⁷⁄₃₂" straight chisel

⅜" straight chisel

⅜" bull-nose chisel

⅛" U-gouge

⅛" dogleg chisel

⅜" dogleg chisel

### Other Tools and Supplies

Copies of the pattern to fit the board

Band saw, scroll saw, or coping saw

Drill with ½" bit (optional)

Bench hook or bracing board

Pencil

Ink pen

Carbon paper

Rubber bands

Compass

Ruler or straightedge

Scissors

Toothbrush for dusting

Very soft brush

Heavy terry cloth towel

Leather carving glove

Fine-grit riffler with a rounded tip

220- and 360-grit sandpaper

Sanding blocks or sanding pads (with foam backs),
     220 or 320 grit

Foam-core fingernail files

White artist's erasers

Scrap board

Dogleg clamps

Depth gauge (note card and scissors, if making one)

Masking tape

Air compressor or canned air (optional)

1" or larger brush for wet checks

### Sharpening Tools

Coarse-grit stone, 800 grit

Fine-grit stone, 8,000 grit

Leather strop

Honing compound

### Finishing Materials

Boiled linseed oil

Turpentine, paint thinner, or mineral spirits

1" or larger brush for applying oil

Lint-free cotton cloths

Newspapers

Scrap board

Mixing pan

---

You'll notice in this demonstration that I am not giving you a specific tool in every instance. This omission is deliberate because while I want to give you some guidelines, I also want you to choose the tool that works best for you.

Along those same lines, don't feel that you need to have the exact tools listed on this tools and materials list. If you have a tool that's close to what is listed here, use that tool. Don't go out and buy a tool simply because it's the one listed.

This project is easy to complete with a basic set of tools including a V-tool, a few sizes of round gouges, a wide-sweep gouge, a few straight chisels, and a bench knife. No other tools are required, and you don't need any specific brands or bent shafts for your tools.

# Preparing the Wood Blank

In this first section, we will be sanding and smoothing the wood blank so the pattern can be easily traced. We will also saw the pattern. I use a band saw, but the cutting steps may also be done using a scroll saw or a hand-held coping saw. You can drill holes in the tight curves of the leaf lobes so the outer edges of the Grape Man Wood Spirit are easier to cut with the band saw.

If you do not have access to a saw, consider doing your background areas, the areas outside the leaf pattern, by dropping them below the level of the outside edge of the pattern and then texturing them using a V-tool.

## The Larger Picture

Our goals for this section:

■ Sand the surface for a smooth tracing

■ Trace only the main outlines of the pattern onto the board

■ Drill and cut out the pattern smoothly

■ Do a final sanding to prepare for carving

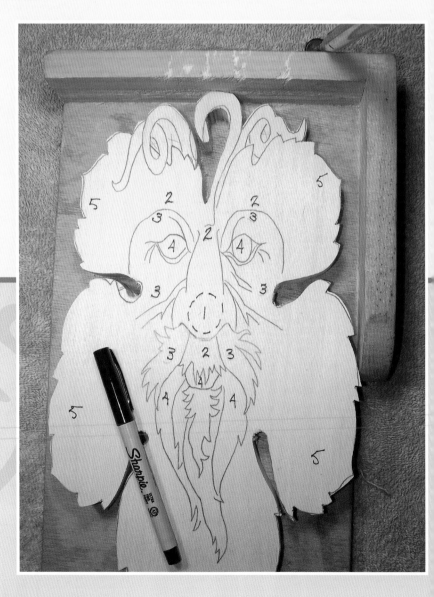

# Tracing the Pattern

For this initial tracing, make sure you get a clean tracing by taking the time to sand the board smooth and ensuring the pattern is secure so it transfers to the wood. Don't worry too much about transferring the little details, however. We'll address those items in later sections.

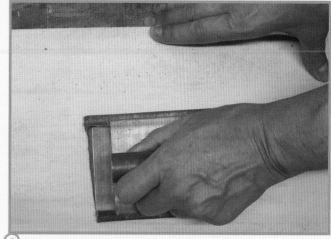

**1** Choose a board of basswood approximately 9" x 14" x 1". Give the wood a good sanding, removing any major saw ridges, grain line ridges, or other imperfections with 220-grit sandpaper on all four sides. You want to create a surface smooth enough for easy tracing of the pattern.

**2** Copy the pattern so it fits the board and use rubber bands to hold it in place. Use as many sheets of carbon paper as needed to cover the board. Trace the main outlines of each area using an ink pen, and check a corner to make sure the carbon is transferring. Because much of the wood will be rough cut, don't spend time tracing all the details at this point.

**3** Check the pattern to make sure everything has transferred. Then, remove the rubber bands, the pattern, and the carbon paper.

## Tip

Print off several copies of the pattern. You'll need extra copies to cut the patterns into pieces later for retracing specific areas.

## Drilling and Cutting the Pattern

To cut the wood spirit's outline from the wood blank, I am using a drill and a band saw. As you work, please follow the common safety techniques and rules that come with your machinery. Safety glasses and ear plugs should be standard equipment in your workshop.

**4** Mark drill holes with a pencil to prepare for band sawing the blank at the four areas where the leaf lobes come close to each other and the tight area in the upper stem. Drilling these holes allows the band saw to cut curves that would otherwise be too tight. If you are using a scroll saw or a coping saw, you may not need to drill holes.

**5** Place a scrap board under the wood to protect the workbench, and lock both boards in place with dogleg clamps. When the boards are secure, put a ½" bit in your largest drill and drill the holes you marked in Step 4.

**6** Sand the back of the board again to remove any chips or splinters caused by the drill. Those chips can catch while sawing, so always sand the back as well.

**7** Get rid of the excess wood along the edges of the pattern with a band saw, a scroll saw, or a coping saw by cutting about ¼" to ½" beyond the pattern lines.

## Tip

Always start a project with a well-sanded surface. Smooth surfaces are safer when you're cutting rough outs with power tools, like a band saw or a scroll saw. Splinters, chips, and rough ridges can easily cause the wood to drag during cutting, which puts you in danger. A smooth surface also gives you a much cleaner tracing for your early pattern work

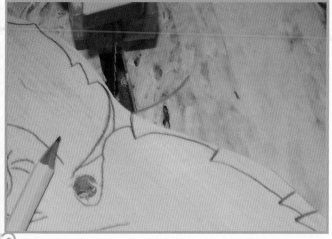

**8** Cut into the angles or corners in one direction first. Then, come back and do the second side of the angle in a second cut. I made pencil marks where I intend to open up the leaf overlaps. This process eliminates the need for a scroll saw, which has a smaller blade that can get into tighter spaces.

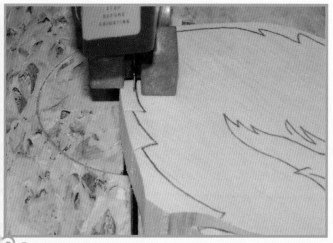

**9** Here you can see the two cuts that make an angle. By cutting in from the edge of the angle to the center, I avoid having to make a sharp turn with the band saw. Notice that my hands are so well out of the way that you can't see them in the photo.

**10** "Walk the band saw" into an inner angle. Remember, this phrase means to make a cut, back up a little, and then make another cut right next to the first. This technique allows you to cut out thin slices, and then continue making long cuts.

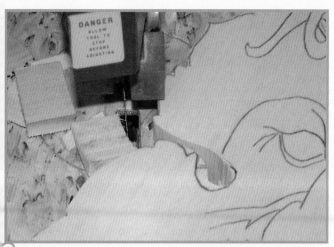

**11** A smooth curve on the cut is more important to me than following the tracing exactly. When the band saw work is done, give both sides of the wood another sanding.

# Roughing Out the Carving

This stage, the roughing-out steps, can also be called "hogging out" or "leveling out." To rough out a pattern means to cut down the elements or groups of elements to a predefined depth in the carving. After these elements are lowered, you return during later steps to smooth them out and add detail. An element is simply one item or object in a pattern. For this project, the eyes, stem, tendrils, mustache, and beard are all individual elements.

There are many ways to approach roughing out, and the style you choose depends on what is comfortable for you. My preference, especially for faces, is to completely rough out all of the areas first, and then come back and dress, or smooth, out the areas to a finished appearance. Using this method, I work each and every area just a bit, in groups related to each other. For example, the eyes need to be deepened before the nose bridge can be cut, and the nose bridge is worked off both the forehead and the nose ball tip.

## The Larger Picture

Our goals for this section:

■ Determine the levels for the elements in the project

■ Create stop cuts between the different elements

■ Rough out all elements of the carving, establishing their initial depth and hogging out excess wood

■ Retrace any pattern areas as needed

■ Rough out the back of the carving to create wall shadows

# Marking the Levels and Making a Stop Cut

Mapping out the levels of any relief pattern makes the work go smoothly and is very easy to do. Keep the mapping to three to five levels. As you begin to sculpture each level later in the work, you can refine how high or low an element moves within that level.

I like to find the highest element first and mark it as Level 1. Then, I search for the lowest points in the design and mark them as Level 5. Level 2 elements lie beneath those in Level 1 but above all the other levels. Level 3 is for elements just below those in Level 2, and Level 4 elements lie just above the background. If you are working on a rectangular design, such as the Tall Celtic Twist (see page 117), mark the background area beyond the design as Level 6. This area will lie below all of the design.

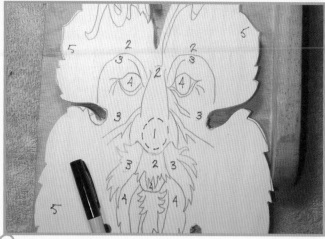

**1** Mark the levels, with 1 being the highest and 5 being the lowest. This numbering system determines how high—or low—each area is in relation to the areas surrounding it. The ball tip of the nose is the highest point, Level 1, on the face. Please follow the mapping on the pattern for all areas of the carving.

**2** Using a chip carving knife or a bench knife, make a stop cut along the outer edges of the nose.

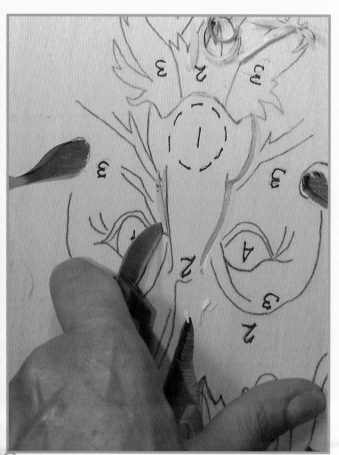

**3** Make another cut, angling the knife away from the nose so the tip of the knife cuts in to the depth of the first cut. This cut will pop out a V-shaped chip. This process widens the stop cut so the round gouge can be used to rough out the cheek areas later.

## Tip

The stop cut is a very simple but extremely useful technique in any relief carving. Along any definable area where one section of the design intersects another area or the background, the stop cut helps you establish the different layers of work. This cut literally stops the gouge from cutting into the defined section or element in the pattern.

## Roughing Out the Eyes and Beard

The face work begins by lowering the areas of the face surrounding the nose, nose beard, and mustache. We will be using a bench knife or a chip carving knife to create stop cuts along the edge of the nose and beard and then a large round gouge to rough out the surrounding areas that lie below the nose area.

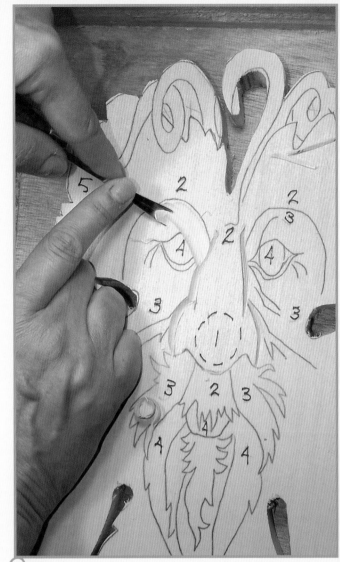

4 Use a large round gouge to begin hogging out the eyes, cheeks, and beard area. I work the gouge from the outer side of the face in to the stop cut along the nose.

### Tip

Work the mustache and beard areas as units, not as individual hairs. This makes it much easier. As we work through the roughing-out steps for the beard, mustache, and lip beard, note how each area is treated as if it were one solid unit.

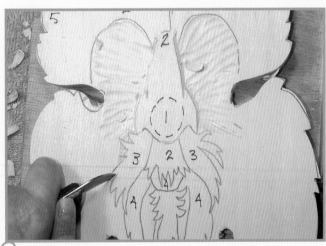

5 Drop the entire eye area to about ¼" deep, tapering it down from the brow into the nose area. Along each of the tight angles made by the mustache hairs, use a bench knife or a chip carving knife to make a small chip cut. This is a three-step cut, as you'll see in the next steps.

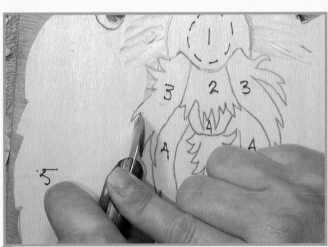

6 To make a triangle-shaped chip, angle the knife toward the center of the V and make a cut. The second cut goes along the other side, also angling in to the center of the V.

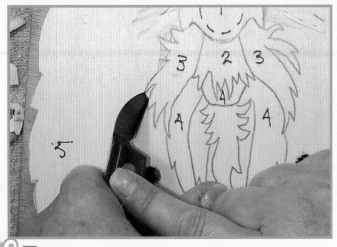

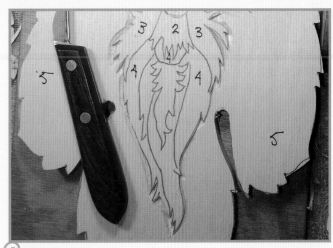

**7** Make the third cut by holding the knife low on the wood and slicing into the other two cuts, removing a small triangle of wood. Chip cut all the beard and mustache angles.

**8** Cut a wide stop cut along the remaining beard lines (see Steps 2 and 3 on page 43).

## Tip

Throughout this demonstration, I give you very few specific depths for the levels. That's because the depth of each element needs to be adjusted according to how thick your original wood is. For example, if I am working on 1"-thick wood and you are working on 3/4"-thick wood, my depth measurements could cause you to carve completely through your wood. Make sure you double-check and adjust the depth of your work as needed before carving to specific depths.

**9** Lower the areas outside the beard with the round gouge. We are not working the inner lines of the mustache, nose beard, or large beard at this point; instead, we are treating this area as a whole. I am working about ¼" deep at this point. Use the chip carving knife or the bench knife to clean up the excess wood left by the round gouge.

## Roughing Out the Leaf Levels

Next, we'll lower the leaf areas and rough them out. In this project, the deepest cut is about one-third of the thickness of the wood.

**10** Along the edge of the board, mark how deep your cuts will go with a compass. Set the compass to the correct length, about one-third of the thickness of the wood. Let the point leg of the compass drop over the back of the board. As you pull the compass, the leg will mark a line at the right depth on the edge of the wood. The back side of the board is at the top of the photo.

**11** Hog out the leaf areas of the project with a wide-sweep gouge. I am working from the ridge that remains after cutting down the beard areas toward the outer edge of the leaf. I'll use that compass line on the sides to check that I don't cut too deep.

## Tip

Because carvings can cup and warp over time, I try to leave at least one-third of the original wood thickness at any point in the carving. Cupping and warping is just part of the nature of wood and its grain as it adjusts to weather and age. By leaving at least a one-third thickness, I am able to minimize the possibility of warping.

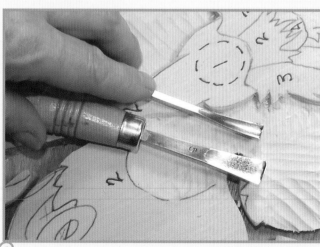

**12** Using the large round gouge to hog out the area and the wide-sweep gouge to smooth out the area, drop the three lower leaf lobes into position. The cutting strokes on the outer edges of the lobes are worked toward the edge of the board to create a natural rounding in the center of the leaf area. Work all three of the lower leaf lobes during this step.

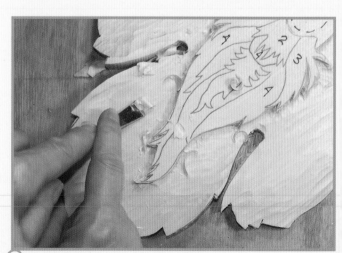

**13** Go back over the surface of the leaves with the wide-sweep gouge to clean up some of the rough ridges left from hogging out the wood.

**14** 14 Take some areas of the leaf down to the compass mark; leave other areas high. This will help make the leaf area roll later in the carving.

## Tip

When planning a carving like the Grape Man Wood Spirit, make sure there is something of interest throughout the entire carving. This includes the edges of the leaves. Pick a few areas along the edge of the leaf that will be dropped to the deepest level of the carving. Accent these areas by picking other sections that will be at the highest level of wood. The outer edges of this carving are just as important to the finished effect as the Grape Man Wood Spirit's face. Notice in the photo that one section of the lower lobe and one edge section of the leaf lobe above it have been left uncarved, as high as the nose area of the design.

**15** Set a depth gauge to the thickness of the wood, 1" in this case, to check your progress. Lay a ruler, or other flat object, across two areas of uncarved wood. Here, that's the nose area and the edge of the lowest leaf lobe. When I place the gauge into the carved areas, I can mark where it touches the edge of the ruler and know how deep I am.

# Making a Depth Gauge

A small piece of cardboard or heavy weight paper can easily be transformed into a depth gauge. This simple tool allows you to measure accurately how deep each area is set into the carving and compare the depth of one area to another.

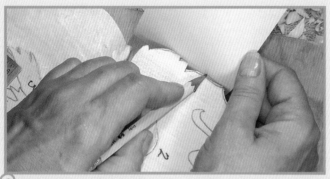

**1** Hold a note card upright on the table next to your piece of wood. Mark the wood's original thickness on the note card with a pencil. If you are working with a ¾" board, this mark will be at ¾" on the note card.

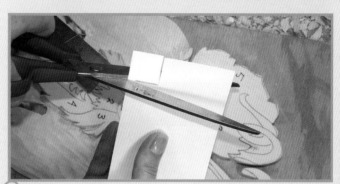

**2** Using scissors, cut in along the mark you made, and then make a second cut to remove the corner of the note card.

**3** Cut the remaining edge to a tapered point.

**4** Use a ruler to draw a line at the top of the notch. This line serves as a quick visual reference for how deep or thick the original wood is.

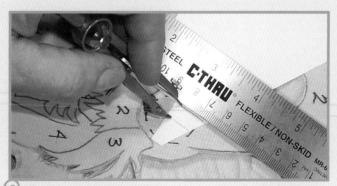

**5** Mark the deepest cut on your note card gauge by drawing a line with the compass you set in Step 10. If any of the carving touches this line, you have reached the deepest point. There is no accidental carving through to the other side!

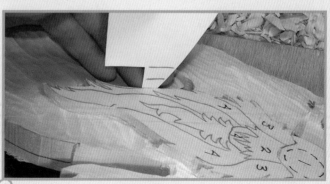

**6** Hold the gauge in place to see how much more wood you need to remove or to check if elements (like the eyes) are carved to the same depth.

# Lowering the Central Stem

The central stem of the Grape Man Wood Spirit has the most dramatic level changes of all of the elements in the design. The stem originates from below the upper leaf lobes at Level 5 and reaches Level 1 where the tendrils curl on top of each leaf lobe.

## Tip

When creating a stop cut, I have more control over the bench knife when pulling the knife toward me. If the cut is made with a gouge, work the tool by pushing the gouge away from you. Keep the cuts—gouge or knife—going in the direction that gives you the most control.

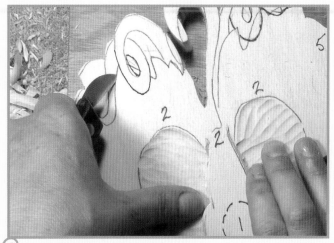

**16** Make the first cut of a wide stop cut along the pattern outlines for the tendrils and tendril curls with the bench knife or the chip carving knife.

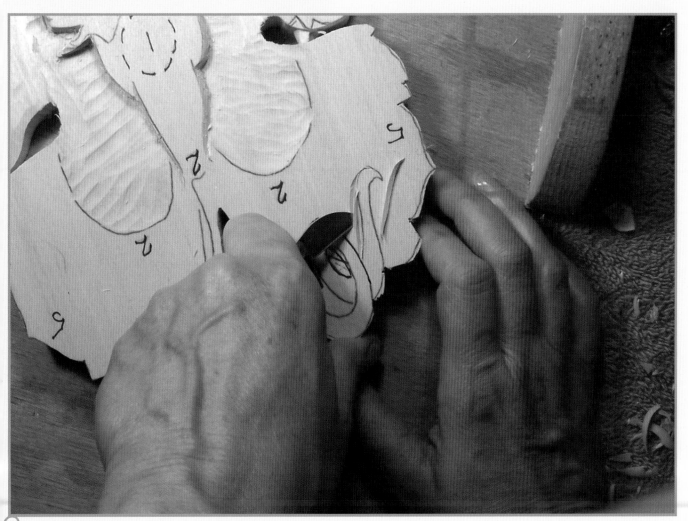

**17** Turn the project and make the second cut of the wide stop cut.

**18** Continue to use the bench knife or the chip carving knife for the stop cuts; use the large round gouge for the roughing out. You want the central stem to be the deepest; then, the leaf will tuck down under the tendril curls.

**19** Check that the stem has been dropped down to the deepest level. My stem matches both the side compass line and the depth gauge line.

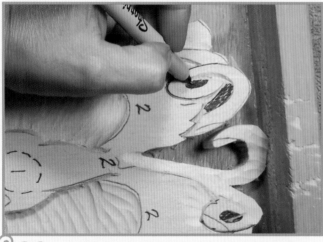

**20** Mark the deep areas that are trapped inside the tendril curls. Marking these extra-deep spaces shows me where I want to make my next very deep, wide stop cut.

## Tip

Patterns are meant as guidelines only. Don't hesitate to make changes in any pattern or design. You can easily add elements, remove elements, or change the dimension of a design to make it unique.

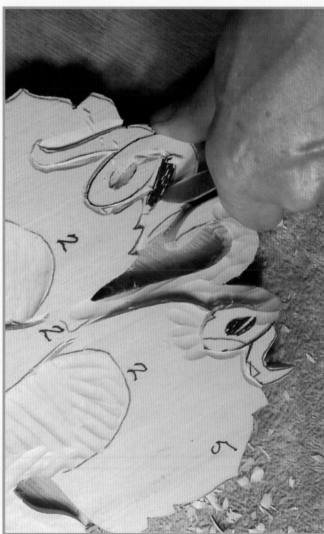

**21** Make angled cuts on both sides of the deep areas with the bench knife. Point the knife toward the center of each open space, popping out a neat, small chip. You can deepen these openings as you need to when you lower the tendrils and the leaf to their levels.

# Working the Brow Ridge and Tendrils

The second highest point in this carving will be the brow ridge, so everything in the upper leaf lobes is carved down from that brow ridge line to a deep point at the tendrils.

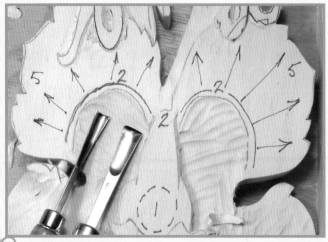

22 Mark the surface of your carving with a pencil to show the change in elevation from 2 (highest) to 5 (lowest). Gently lower the leaf from the brow ridge to a deep point at the tendrils with the large round gouge and the wide-sweep gouge.

23 As you work the upper leaf lobes, you will come to a tight spot in the corner created by the tendrils. Use the bench knife along the tendril lines to cut a thin stop cut. Then, use a small round gouge to lift the corner out.

24 Find a gouge that matches the curves of the tendrils. For example, this large round gouge has a profile that is a half circle. Upend the gouge and push it straight into the wood to make a stop cut where the tendril curves tightly.

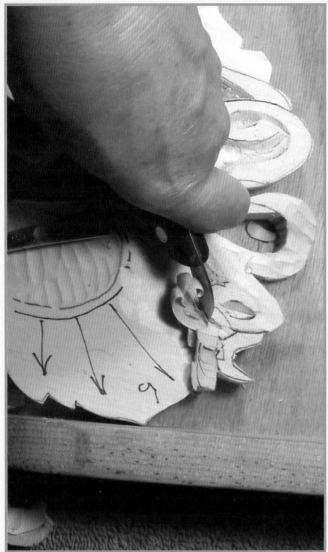

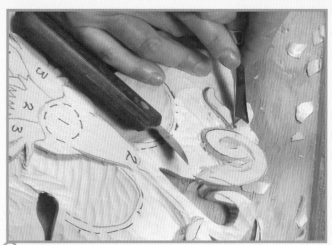

**26** Tuck the tendril curls. Use a stop cut along the pattern line, and then carve into that stop cut with the round gouge.

**25** Repeat the stop cuts as necessary. I often do roughing-out work in two repeated stages. I stop cut with the bench knife along the pattern line, and then I go into the stop cut with my gouges, which sometimes slightly deepen the original stop cut. I use the bench knife or chip carving knife to remove any chips not freed by the previous two cuts.

**27** Drop the tendril level by using a straight chisel. Upend the tool on its profile and push a nice, deep stop cut to neatly finish the end of the tendril.

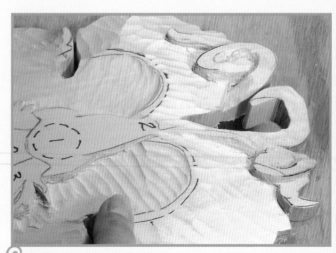

**28** Check your work before you move on. The tendrils should be lower than the leaf lobes and at the deepest level.

# Retracing Pattern Sections

When the roughing-out work was done inside the eye area, the carving removed the pattern lines. By cutting the eye section from your pattern with scissors, you can retrace the eye details for the next stages of work. Retracing small sections of a pattern is a common step with any relief project.

**29** Smooth the eye area with the wide-sweep gouge in preparation for retracing the eyes. Gently carve away any ridges left by the gouge during the roughing-out stage. You want this area smooth enough to easily retrace the eye details. Cut the eye area, including the cheek lines, from another copy of the pattern.

## Tip

Especially with relief landscapes and wildlife scenes, retracing parts of the pattern is very important. First, determine the different levels in your landscape—background, middle ground, and foreground—and rough carve each area to the desired depth. Then, cut the pattern in pieces that match those same levels. Include all of the elements that fall into that level. As an example, when you retrace the background of a landscape, it might include the clouds and sky area, the distant mountain range, and the pines along the foothills. Retracing avoids the more complicated method of trying to keep the excess and detail pattern lines during the roughing-out stages.

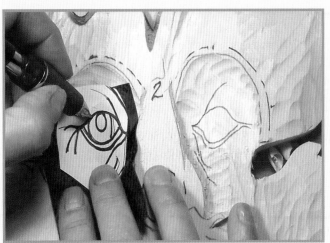

**30** Place the cut pattern pieces on your project, tape them down, and slip a small piece of carbon paper underneath. Retrace the lines using an ink pen.

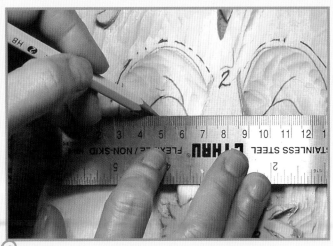

**31** Use a straightedge or a ruler to check that each eye is in the correct position. The eyes should line up along the corners in a straight line that dissects the nose bridge.

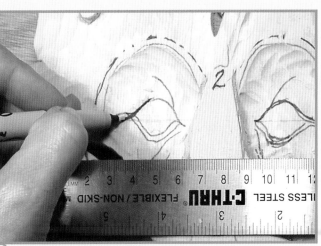

**32** Re-mark the eye corners to bring the tracing lines into adjustment. Notice that the outer corner of the left eye on my project was too high and needed to be changed.

# Carving the Eyes

During this carving section, we will work the eye area of the face. This includes dropping the eyeball level to the deepest point of the carving as well as sculpturing the eyelids and eye pads above and below the eye.

Remember, the eye is the deepest element in a face carving, whether the face is a front view or a profile. The eye is a ball over which the eyelids must be able to close. The upper eyelid lies higher than the lower lid, the lower lid is tucked down into the carving. The outer corner of the eye, near the hairline, is slightly deeper than the corner next to the nose because of the curvature of the face. The edge of the top eyelid falls where the nose bridge lies.

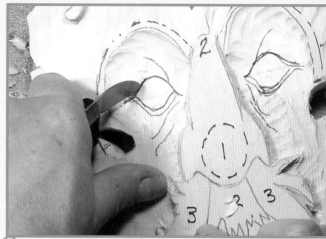

**33** Cut a stop cut with the chip carving knife along each eyelid line.

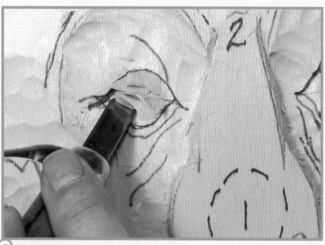

**34** Use a ⅜" bull-nose chisel to lower the eyeball area. Work from the center of the eyeball toward the eyelids with your chisel.

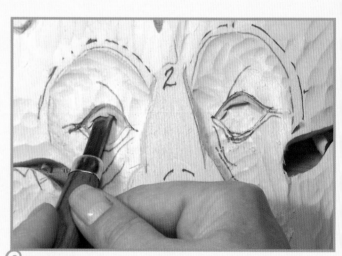

**35** Repeat Step 35 several times until the eyeball is shaved to a nice depth and a nice curve.

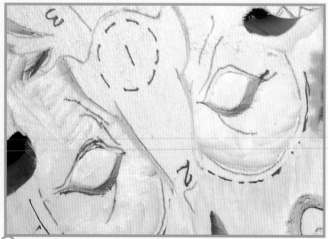

**36** Lower the eye area until it is at the correct depth on your gauge. Notice how deep I dropped the eye area.

## Tip

The straight chisel is excellent for working the eye areas, but it often leaves deep scratches along the edge of the profile in the cut. By rounding the edges of a straight chisel when you sharpen it, you can get rid of these scratch marks. Over time, the rounded edges will develop into a slightly rounded profile, which just makes it perfect for relief carving. Don't do this to a straight chisel if you only have one in your kit or to your favorite straight chisel. But as your tool collection grows, find an older, rarely used chisel and turn it into a bull-nose one.

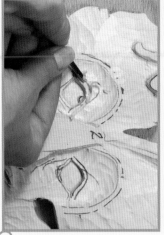

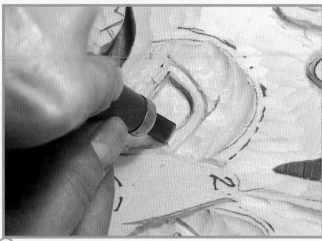

**37** Draw a line where you want the upper eyelid, about ⅛" away from the eyeball area. Using a V-tool , cut along the lid line. The eyelid will be slightly lower than the brow area above it. Cut both sets of eyelids, top and bottom, with the V-tool.

**38** Upend the chisel to create a straight stop cut at the intersection, or corner, of the eye to separate the upper and lower eyelids.

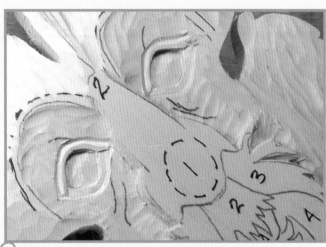

**39** Drop the level of the entire lower lid below that of the upper one with the ⅜" bull-nose chisel.

**40** Do a visual check of the face to this point. Looking from the forehead down, the brow ridge is high, the upper lid drops, the eyeball is the deepest, and the lower lid is deeper than the upper lid.

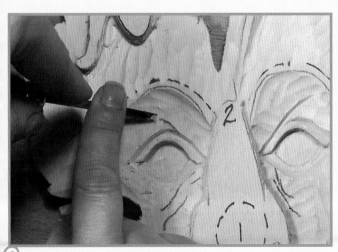
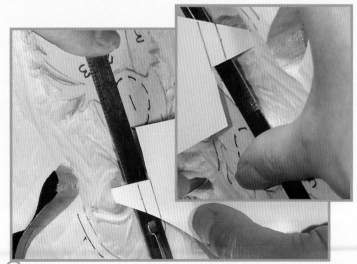

**41** Outline the fold line in the upper brow area with the V-tool.

**42** Recheck the eye depth. The eyes should be the carving's deepest point. The depth gauge shows I have plenty of room to drop the eyes more. Repeat Steps 34 to 42 until the eyeball area is at the gauge-mark level.

# Creating the Eye Pupils

There are a lot of ways to create the pupil area of a face carving. If you plan to paint the face, the pupils can simply be colored instead of carved into the eyeball. Some carvers mark the pupil area with a shallow V-tool line. Because I am not going to paint this carving, I will carve out the pupil area. A carved pupil creates a natural black shadow in the face, giving the pupil a realistic look.

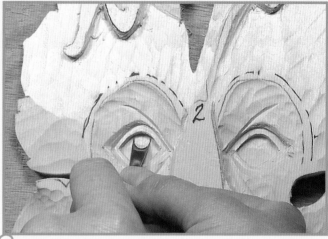

**43** Use the large round gouge and gently walk it into the pupil area at an angle pointed toward the forehead. This cut, when finished, will be below the deepest gauge mark, so work carefully. Notice that the pupil is not a full circle: It's a half circle tucked into the upper eyelid.

**44** Free the large round gouge cut with the bench knife or the chip carving knife.

**45** Notice how creating the pupil with the gouge forces the pupil area to become deeply shadowed, exactly like the human eye. This carving process makes the pupil quick, easy, and always round!

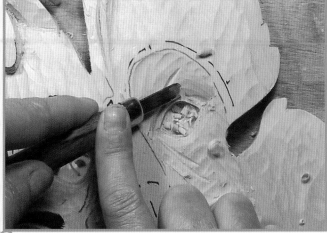

**46** Round the bottom edge of the area above the upper eyelid with a chisel.

## Shaping the Eyelids

It's important to follow the grain of the wood in this area. Work from the center of the lid toward the outer corner.

**47** Work from the center of the lid out to the corner of the eye.

### Tip

All of the grain is running from the top of the face toward the bottom leaf point, as marked on the left. This means that if I cut the eyelid areas in one stroke, half of the cut is going into the grain. Working into the grain means that the wood can break, or chip out, or the tool can get caught and pull too deeply into the cut. By working from the center of the lid out, as marked on the right, I am always carving with the grain, so there are no chip outs.

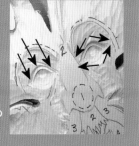

**48** Do the same for the area below the lower eyelid. These steps connect the face to the eye. Use the 3/8" bull-nose chisel with the tool held upside down to shave the upper cheek areas to a smooth finish. Cut the two wrinkle lines in the cheek area with the V-tool.

# Working the Mustache

The beard of our Grape Man Wood Spirit is separated into four units. The first is the small mustache directly under the nose; the second is made up of the two side pieces of the mustache. The little beard under the lower lip and the large beard area that reaches toward the bottom leaf lobe make up parts three and four.

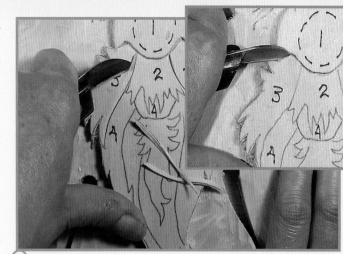

**49** Use the chip carving knife to cut a thin, one-cut stop cut along the pattern line at the base of the nose. Make a wide stop cut under the nose and along the mustache areas. We will drop the mustache under the nose; the stop cut will be the demarcation line.

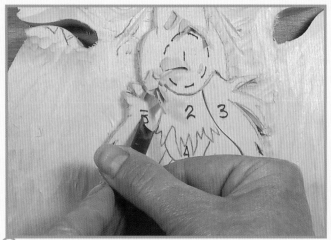

**50** Because the ball of the nose is the highest area of the carving, and wood cannot be added to make the nose higher, lower the areas surrounding the nose. Use any chisel to remove wood.

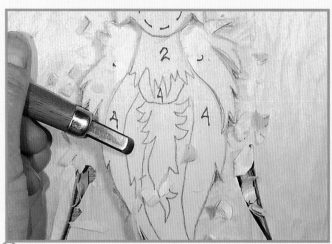

**51** Take the outer left side and the outer right side of the mustache to the level of the surrounding cheek areas where the inside corners of the mustache touch the nose. Leave the outer corners of the mustache area slightly proud of, or higher than, the cheek areas.

**52** Lower the center area of the mustache. Use the ⅜" bull-nose chisel to make the cuts, and then use the bench knife or the chip carving knife to free the chips.

**53** Chip cut along the points of the mustache. Make the three cut to pop out neat, small triangles along the mustache edge.

**54** Notice that the chip cuts free up those sharp corners so you can shape the rest of the mustache area.

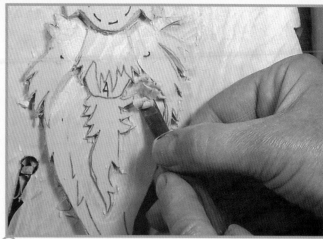

**55** Use the wide-sweep gouge, the large round gouge, and/or the ⅜" bull-nose chisel to tuck the outer mustache hair below the small mustache under the nose. Choose the tool that best fits the space between the side mustaches and the chin beard.

**56** Check your work before you move on. Note that the eyes are at the deepest level, and the nose ball and eyebrow ridge are still at the original level of the wood. The mustache has been tucked under the nose but is not quite as deep as the eyes. From the nose, the mustache flares back to the original wood level.

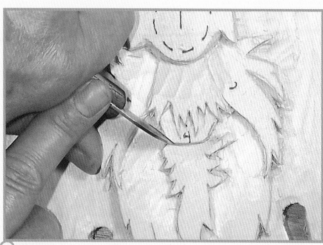

**57** Chip cut the mustache where it overlays the lip, and then work the small mustache under the nose. I start with a thin stop cut and then use the chisel or the wide-sweep gouge to lower this small mustache beneath his lower lip.

**58** Make a stop cut along the upper edge of the mustache, and then lower the lip slightly below that mustache area. Next, stop cut the small mustache under the nose and lower it below the lip.

## Tip

I prefer to work any hair areas as complete units first. For example, I work the beard as one unit and the mustache as one unit. This lets me drop a group of hair into its correct level in the carving. Once the general shape is established, I can divide the unit into sculptured or shaped clusters of strands with my V-tool and chisel. During the smoothing steps, I will add individual hairs to each strand with the V-tool.

## Shaping the Nose

The body of the nose is a half cylinder that is wider at the bottom and narrower at the top by the eyes. You don't want a hard edge joint on the sides of the nose where they meet the cheeks, so soften the joints by using a round gouge. Don't use a V-tool or make a stop cut that is too hard. As you are working, remember to visualize the three half circles of the nose: the ball tip and the two nostrils. The ball tip lies on top of the cylinder, and the nostrils lie beside the cylinder. Round all three with the bench knife or the large straight chisel.

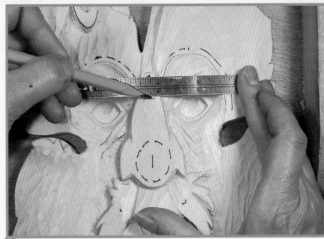

**59** Lay the straightedge across the highest points of the upper eyelids and make a mark on the nose with a pencil. This mark shows where the nose bridge lies on the face. The angle between the forehead and nose bridge is very sharp and steep but not very long.

**60** Use the ⅜" bull-nose chisel to cut into the pencil mark for the nose bridge, working down from the forehead area.

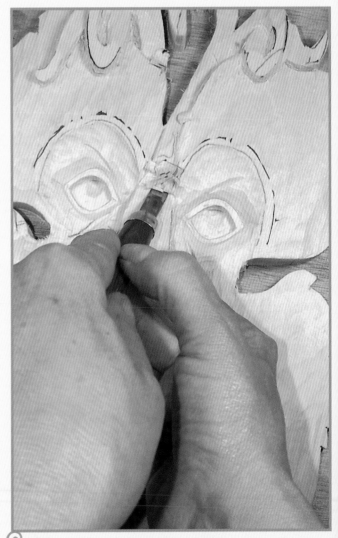

**61** Cut the second side of the angle, working from the nose toward the forehead, stopping at the nose bridge angle. Clean up the joint line in the forehead-nose angle.

**62** Do a depth check. You can see in the close-up that the bridge is about one-half of the wood depth between the original wood level and the depth of the eyes.

**63** Use the wide-sweep gouge to taper the nose ridge into the forehead-bridge angle. Start the cut at the top of the nose ball and work toward the nose bridge.

**64** Use the ⅜" bull-nose chisel or the straight chisel to round the tip of the nose, tapering it toward the mustache.

## Tip

Place the center joint of your finger on the bridge of your nose. Now, blink your eyes a few times. You can feel that the lashes of your upper eyelid are right underneath your finger. This is the correct placement of the nose bridge in relation to the upper eyelid.

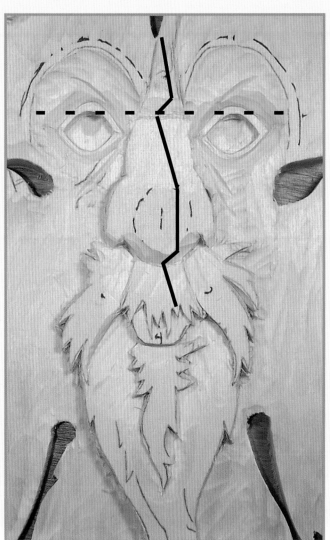

**65** Map out the level flow through the nose. Notice that the nose actually begins in the forehead area just above the nose bridge. The nose bridge dips quickly. The straight of the nose rises to the nose ball, the highest point in your carving. The bottom edge of the nose ball drops at a steep angle into the small mustache under the nose.

## Creating Wall Shadows

The roughing-out stages of a relief carving may include some work on the back of the board. To create dramatic shadows against the wall when the project is hung, the outer edges of the back are carved to lift those edges of the wood away from the wall.

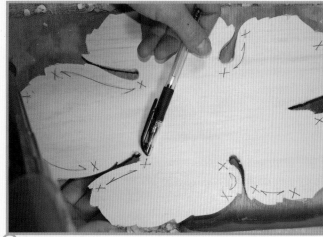

**66** Find the areas along the leaf edge that were left higher during the roughing-out work on the leaf lobes on the face of the wood. Turn the carving over and mark those thick edges along the back of the outer leaf with a pencil.

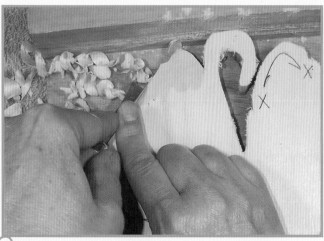

**67** Round over the thick leaf edges on the back of the carving to create shadows on the wall when the carving is hung. These areas will cast shadows that make the leaf look as if it curls. Use both the wide-sweep gouge and the ⅜" bull-nose chisel.

### Tip

At this point, only a few parts of the front of the carving are at the original wood level, so it will rock when you work the back. Grab something soft to use as wedges or braces. I chose pencil erasers. It is extremely important that the carving stay still because rocking can cause the knife to slip. The weird-shaped blue eraser in the center is a kneaded eraser, which works well because you can pull it apart into small pieces and mold it to any shape.

**68** The roughing-out stage of this carving is complete!

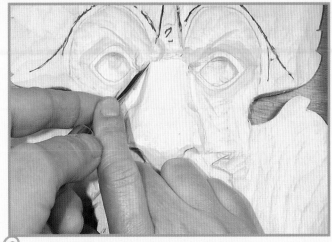

## Joining the Eye and Nose Bridge

At the nose bridge area of the face, the nose, eyes, and upper eyelids intersect along the side of the nose. Although this is a very small area of the overall face, developing the wrinkles of the eyelid and details of the eye corner at that intersection adds realism to your carving's features.

**14** Smooth the joint between the nose and the cheek using a V-tool. Don't make a deep V-cut; instead, glide the V-tool along the joint just enough to clean both sides of the area.

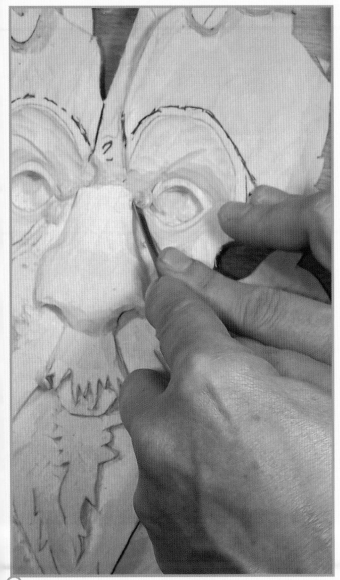

**15** Work the corner area of the other eye using the V-tool.

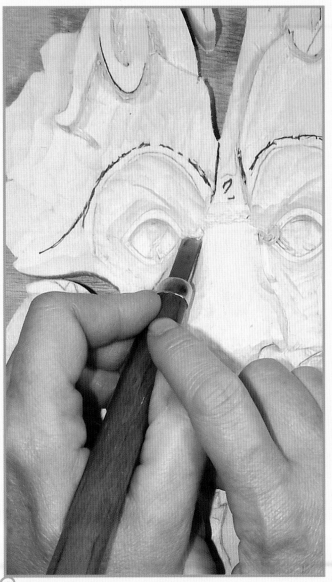

**16** Free the V-tool chip with the chisel.

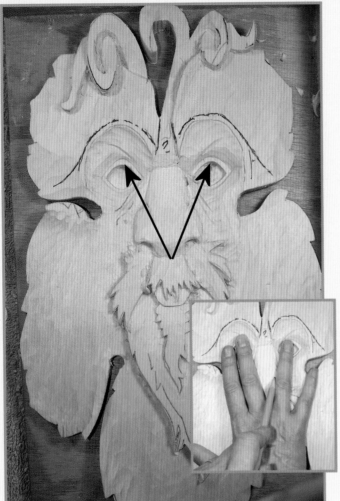

## Establishing the Nostril's Sides

The nostrils are small half-sphere shapes that lie along the ball tip of the nose. The angle of the intersection is determined by a line drawn between the eye pupil and the center of the upper lip.

**17** Mark the nostril angle with a pencil. To estimate the angle, put the top of the palm of your hand on your upper lip and your fingertips over the pupils of your eyes. The angle of your open fingers is the same angle of the nostrils where they roll away from the nose. The nostril lines on my carving are in line with the angle created when I used my fingers as a guide.

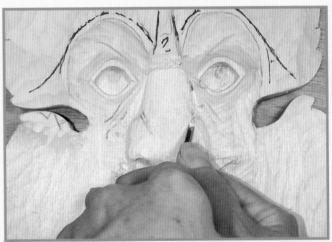

**18** Use the V-tool to carve the nostril angle. Notice that it starts about halfway into the nostril and ends at the upper cheek.

**19** Check the carving from the side. The eyeball should be the lowest point of the face, and the upper eyelids and eye corner should flow into the intersection at the nose. The nostrils now have their dark shadowed nostril holes and have been blended into the nose ball tip with the addition of the nostril angle lines.

**20** Use the V-tool to create the two wrinkles in the cheek area under the eyes.

# Working the Eyelid Pads and Cheeks

With the basic sculpturing completed in the eye, eyelid, nose, and cheek areas finished, it is time to refine the curves and detailing. We will be reworking all of these sections to smooth any rough surfaces and round over the curved areas.

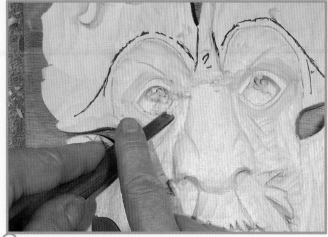

**21** Begin smoothing the cheek areas with the ⅜" bull-nose chisel or the wide-sweep gouge. Watch the direction of the grain—always try to carve with the grain. Change or move the position of the carving often so that you get a clean approach to your strokes.

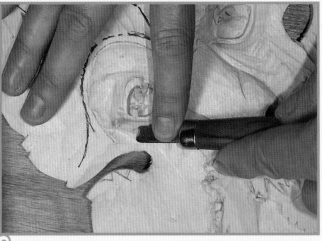

**22** Smooth the lower cheek area that leads up to the eye corner. Use the chisel to make a crisp but very shallow stop cut at the joint line between the cheek and the upper eyelid.

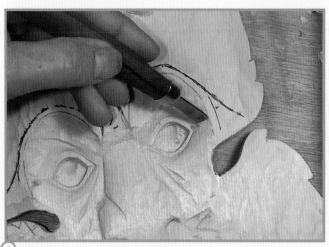

**23** Where the upper eye pads or eyelid meet the lower eyelid at the outer corner of the eye, use the ⅜" bull-nose chisel to create a crisp joint line. Later, when I do the smoothing steps on the eye area, I will turn this crisp line into two or three crow's feet wrinkles.

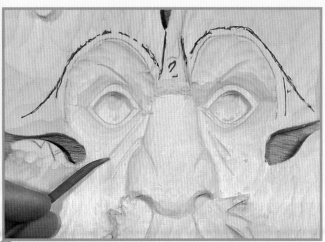

**24** Take a moment to check the cheek wrinkles that were added in Step 20 on page 68. On my carving, the wrinkles don't match on both sides of the nose. Generally, that's okay because a face does not wrinkle evenly or in a pattern, but I am going to make an adjustment.

**25** I added a line on each side: one on the top on the left side and one on the bottom on the right side. Then, I cut them using the V-tool. This gives me the balanced, or mirrored, look that I want.

26 Once you have adjusted the wrinkles to your satisfaction, add new wrinkle lines with the V-tool. Recut the old wrinkle lines with the same tool.

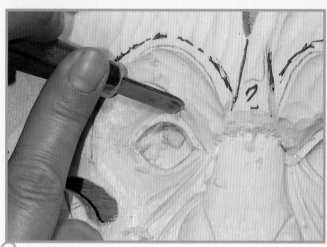

27 Clean up and smooth the upper eyelids and upper eye pad areas. My carving needs some special attention at the joint of the eyelid and the upper eye pad area where I have a deep gouge stroke.

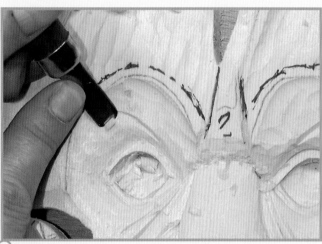

28 I smoothed out the deep gouge mark so that the two areas blend together.

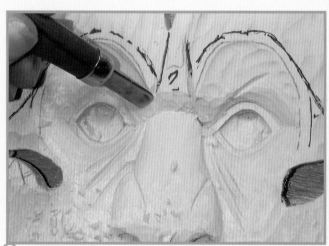

29 Treat the bottom angle of the nose bridge as part of the upper eye pad. I want these two areas to flow together without a ridge or a break.

## Tip

Try one of these four techniques, or a combination of them, to smooth the carving.
1) Chip carving knife or bench knife. Lay the tool flat against the wood surface to gently shave away ridges.
2) Bull-nose chisel. Turn the tool over and work with the back edge of the blade to remove thin bits of wood.
3) Bull-nose chisel or straight chisel. Hold the tool high on its cutting edge to scrape away ridges.
4) Sandpaper with 220 to 320 grits. Rub lightly to quickly remove the ridges left from the roughing-out carving. Sandpaper will leave behind fine scratches in the wood surface, so rough-grit sandpapers should be a last resort.

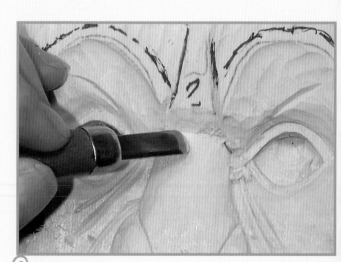

30 Check the crease of the nose bridge for leftover fibers. To clean these up, upend the chisel and use it in a scraping motion. This is a great way to smooth out very hard-to-reach areas to a fine, even finish.

# Creating Eyebrow Hair

Eyebrows on the human face appear as raised areas along the brow ridge. However, when carving wood spirits, eyebrows and other hair, such as beards and mustaches, are most often detailed down into the wood using a V-tool or a chip carving knife.

**49** Mark the eyebrow hairs with a pencil. I don't add many at this point because I can always add more later.

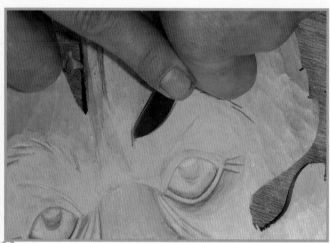

**50** Use the chip carving knife to carve the hair with two slicing cuts in a V-shaped trough. The chip carving knife gives me more control than the V-tool as the brow rolls from the top of the face down toward the chin and from the left to the right.

**51** Clean up the surface of the carving with the white artist's eraser.

**52** Using the chip carving knife, work only a few lines initially to establish the flow of the hair and some different levels or strands in the hair. After the entire project has been completed through the smoothing stage, we will return to these areas to add more detailing.

## Veining the Leaves

Adding the veins to the leaves is done at this point in the carving because the placement of the veins highlights some features of the face. Notice that the center vein of the side leaf lobes joins and becomes one of the wrinkles in the cheek. The center vein of the upper leaf lobes flows and joins the eyebrows.

**53** Mark the leaf veins with a pencil. One set of veins comes from the end of the eyebrow ridge. Another set, the center leaf lobes, comes from one of the cheek wrinkles. This placement helps to connect the face and the leaf.

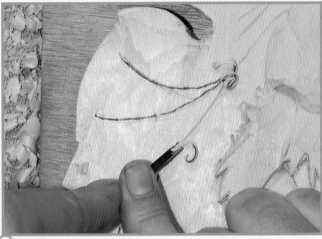

**54** Use the V-gouge and make several cuts to establish the full length of each vein, depending on how that vein moves across the grain. This process prevents the edges of the cut from chipping out.

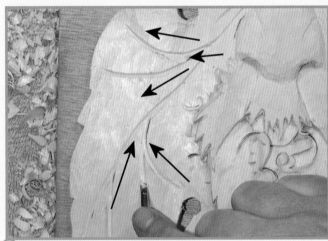

**55** Make several light passes with the V-tool and slowly lower and widen the V-tool line instead of making one hard, deep cut. Work toward the intersection. The arrows on the bottom vein of the leaf go into the joint where the cuts intersect. In the vein above, I worked away from the intersection, and you can see the chip out that occurred.

**56** Use the chisel to roll over the sides of the leaf section into the V-tool cuts you just made. You don't want a flat plane and then a sudden drop into the V-tool stroke. The goal is to create a gentle rolling over of the leaf.

## Tip

With V-tool carving, many of your lines will cut across the grain of the wood, and many of the curved lines within the pattern will begin going with the grain and then slowly change direction. Be sure to use a well-sharpened gouge. If you are using wood with coarse grain, you can pre-cut the line that you are going to carve. Simply score the pattern line with a bench knife to the depth of your final cut. Use several strokes with your V-tool to reach the final depth. Then, lay the chisel point into the score line and begin taking away the wood in shallow layers.

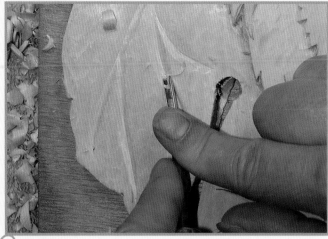

**57** Recut the V-tool cut very lightly to clean up the trench. Work through all five of the leaf lobes, adding the veining and rolling the leaf sections into the veins.

**58** See how the last eyebrow hair has now become the leaf vein.

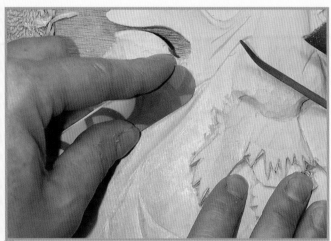

**59** Lightly sand the roll-over areas of the V-tool. Be careful you don't lose the chisel planes in the leaf. I use a variety of tools for this step, including the small riffler, sandpaper that can be folded and pushed into the trench, and foam-core fingernail files.

### Tip

Choose sanding materials based on the area you want to sand. I use fine-grit sandpaper, 220 grit or higher, when I need to reach into deep areas of the work. I fold or roll it so it can go where sanding pads or rifflers don't fit. A riffler keeps the crisp line in the bottom of a V-tool cut. Foam-core emery boards or fingernail files work for a number of things because they can be easily cut into different shapes to fit each area of the carving.

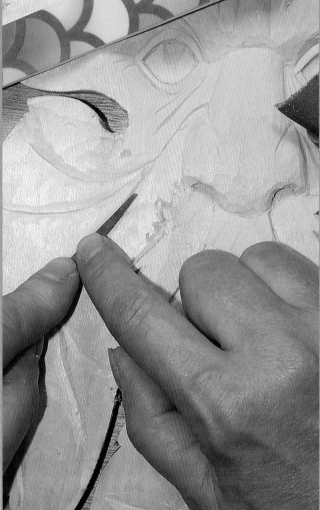

**60** Lower the inside of the V-tool trough with the small riffler.

## Undercutting the Mustache and Beard

Undercuts, made with a chip carving knife and a dogleg chisel, create dark shadows in a relief carving. These dark shadows visually push an area off the wood, giving a deeper, almost three-dimensional, effect to your work.

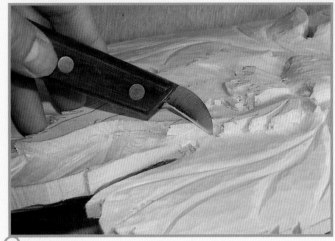

**61** If you have room, undercut the sides of the mustache. Otherwise, simply roll the sides of the mustache down to touch the leaf area.

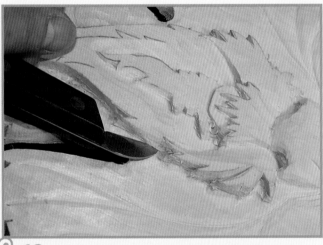

**62** Make the undercuts in two cuts. Laying the chip carving knife almost flat against the wood, make the first cut where the upper element meets the background element. This means the first cut is below the mustache at the level of the leaf.

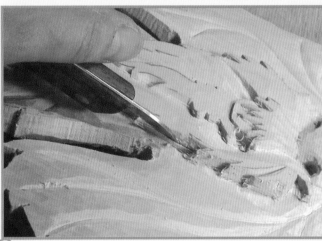

**63** Holding the chip carving knife at an angle, make the second cut about halfway up the wall of the mustache and angled down to meet the first cut. This frees a wedge or triangle of wood and leaves an open space below the top surface of the undercut element.

**64** Free the top of the undercut with the chip carving knife, if needed.

### Tip

There are two great reasons to make undercuts in a relief carving. First, they hide the joint line between two elements. Second, undercuts cast black shadows onto the elements below them, heightening the illusion of depth.

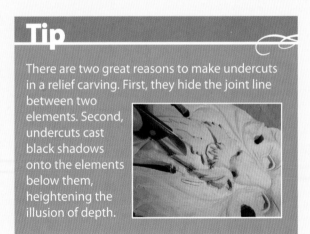

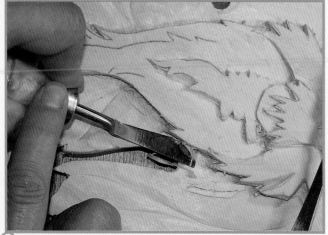

**65** Clean up the undercut with a dogleg chisel so the angle is smooth, even though no one will see it. The shaft angle of this chisel places the cutting edge flat against the wood and is perfect for sliding right into an undercut. You could also use the wide-sweep gouge, the ⅜" bull-nose chisel, or the straight chisel for this step.

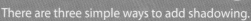
## Tip

There are three simple ways to add shadowing.
1) Add an undercut that tucks the one element beneath the foreground item.
2) Plan several small areas of your design where one element of the pattern lies in the highest level of the design and is surrounded by an area that lies in the deepest area of carving. For example, the deep eyes of the Grape Man Wood Spirit are shadowed by the higher brow ridge.
3) Completely free a small element from the background wood, making it float over the surface of the carving.

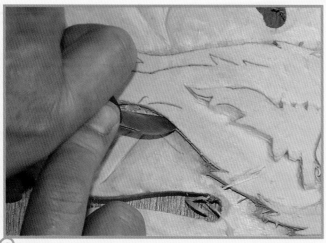

**66** Recut an undercut several times until you have created a strong dark shadow. Clean the joint line between each cutting.

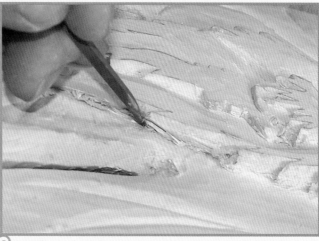

**67** Continue cleaning the undercut. The riffler is another tool that efficiently cleans up the inside area of an undercut.

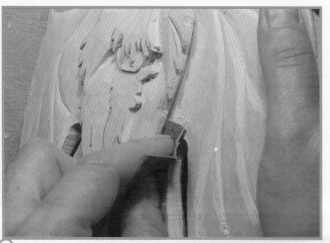

**68** Lightly sand the finished undercut with a folded piece of 220-grit sandpaper.

## Tip

The short walls in an undercut create medium-toned shadows. Deep walls create dark to black shadows. You can use both types, short- and deep-walled cuts, to give the project's shadows variety.

§69 Undercut most, but not all, of the beard area. I decided not to do the areas near the nose and the bottom tip to leave a few spots of soft shadow.

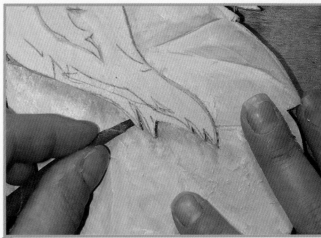

§70 Check your work under a single light source to see the shadows created by the undercuts. For this photo, I turned off all but one light. See how dramatic those undercuts are?

# Dealing with Chip Outs

Chip outs can happen without much provocation in relief carving. Often, the best way to deal with a chip out is to simply carve it away. Medium-size chips can be glued back into place using wood glue. Place a small drop of glue on both the chip and where the chip broke away from the wood. Let the glue begin to set by waiting for about one or two minutes.

Then, place the chip back into position. You may need to hold the chip in place for a few minutes until the glue has set enough to hold it in place. Very large chips may need a small support dowel to carry the weight of the chip when it is glued back into position. I use round wooden toothpicks to create those repair dowels.

## Shaping the Beard

The main features of any wood spirit are his hair and his beard. In the following steps, we will shape, sculpt, and smooth each area of the Grape Man Wood Spirit's beard and mustache in preparation for adding the fine, individual hair cuts.

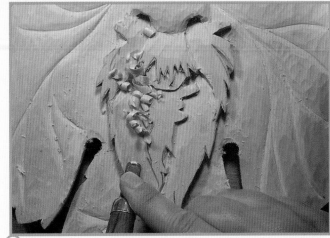

**71** Smooth away the roughing-out ridges on the top surface of the beard and mustache areas with the chisel. I am using the ⅜" bull-nose chisel, but please remember that you may also use the straight chisel or the wide-sweep gouge for any smoothing step.

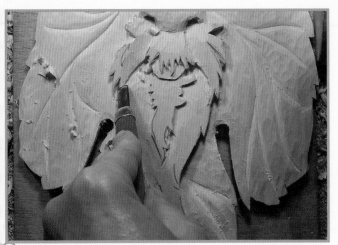

**72** Tuck the top edge of the beard under the level of the mustache. Make a stop cut along this joint line with the chisel from the previous step, and then lower the beard side of the stop cut.

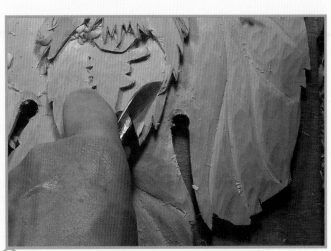

**73** Make a wide stop cut on the other side of the mustache with the bench knife or the chip carving knife, and use the chisel to smooth that wide cut.

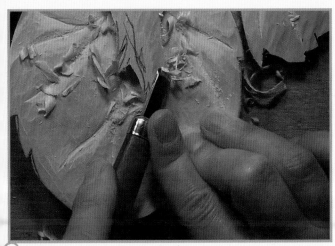

**74** Roll over the outside edge of the hair slightly with the chisel as you smooth the surrounding areas.

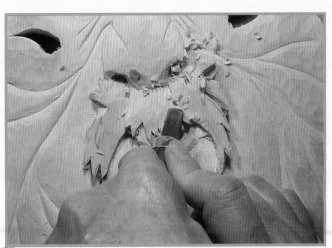

**75** Roll the center of the mustache area sharply into the joints of the side mustache and nose.

**Relief Carving Wood Spirits | 81**

**76** Work the chisel inside the nostril areas as you smooth the side mustache areas. The mustache should flow smoothly out from the nostril without a defining ridge.

**77** Do a quick and light cleanup at this point with the roll of sandpaper, the riffler, and the fingernail file. Don't sand away so much wood that you lose the planed look.

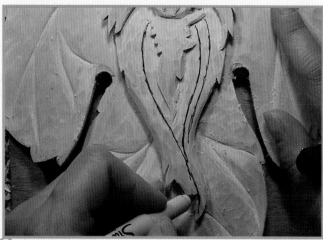

**78** With a pencil, mark new guidelines for any ridge lines that were lost as you lowered the beard and smoothed it out.

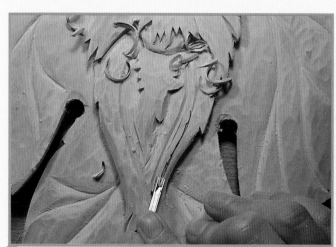

**79** Use the V-tool to create a nice, deep trench along the ridge lines. I want these lines to be strong, so I am going fairly deep with the V-tool.

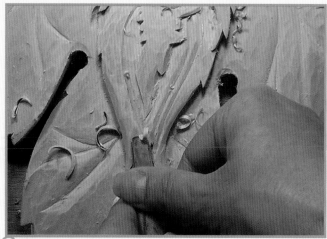

**80** With the chisel, round over the sides of the V-tool trench in the beard ridges.

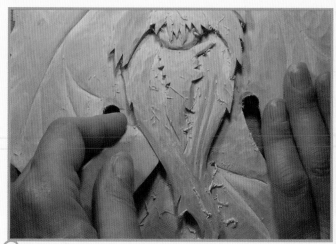

**81** Tuck one side of the new beard ridges under the other side as you round over the trenches, and then tuck the right side of the beard under the left side where they join near the beard tip. Clean up any loose fibers and remaining pencil lines in the beard and undercut areas.

## V-tooling the Hair

The V-tool can be used to create deep trough lines just as we worked in the leaf veins and just as we did to separate different sections of the beard along the higher ridge lines. With light pressure, we will use the V-tool to create the fine, flowing lines of individual hairs.

**82** Start the V-tool work for the mustache and beard hair. Curve your cuts to match the curve of the beard or mustache areas. Remember, you can make one long hair line out of several V-tool cuts.

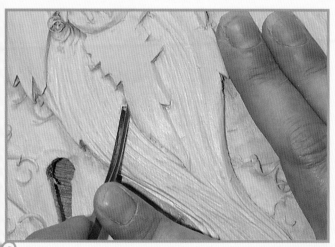

**83** Take the V-tool hair strokes right into the adjacent elements. In this case, that's the lip beard.

**84** Let the V-tool cuts run right into the nose tip, and then go back with the chisel or the chip carving knife to clean up the nose tip. No space or break exists between the start of the mustache hair and the tip of the nose.

**85** Notice how some areas of the beard and mustache change level or height. For those places, it's easiest to cut that hair section into two areas, carving away from the highest point so that each cut is flowing down into the wood.

### Tip

Each and every V-tool cut has a little bit of a curve to it. Try to follow the curve of the area for the curve of the hair. Don't be concerned if the hairs seem to go in every direction. Wood spirits do not have well-trimmed beards, sculptured mustaches, or combed hair.

The best option is to work the hair in lots of short ½"- to 1"-long cuts. I am not attempting to go all the way from his lip to the tip of his beard. As you do more carving, you will learn how to go the whole length with one moving, sweeping, twisting V-tool cut. This hair area has so many ups and downs because of the wide-sweep gouge work in the levels cutting. Remember, any area can have a grain direction change because of the curve of the hair cuts. Short cuts with the V-tool are more controllable than long ones.

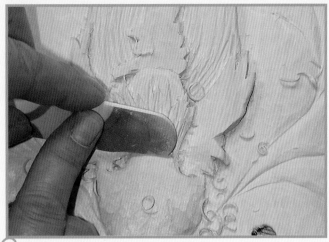

**86** Turn the project upside down to get a new view of the tip of the nose. Clean it up with the fingernail file as needed.

**87** Because of the sweep of the lip beard—low at the lip and high at the tip—do this area in two directions also (see Step 85).

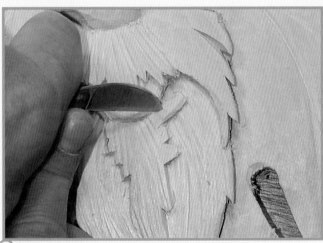

**88** Because the little spit of hair on the lip beard goes completely against the grain, use the chip carving knife and cut the hair with two freestyle chip strokes. This is the first side of the first cut. Note: The V-tool may look easier to use, but it will tear out wood all along that cut.

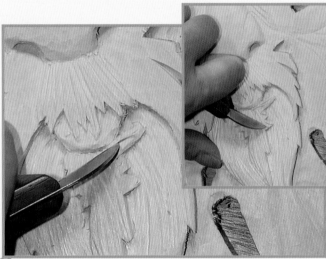

**89** Recut the same line of hair, but this time angle the chip carving knife slightly. The new angle shaves a thin strip out of the first cut and makes a great hair stroke. Do the same type of freestyle chip-cut hairs on the lower pointy beard tips.

## Tip

I turn my project upside down so I can cut the high section of the small mustache under the nose and keep my V-tool cutting in a downward direction. Cutting into a higher level of wood with the V-tool means that your tool digs deep. It will stay with the grain level, and you will find yourself trapped or dug in. If that happens, don't try and push on through the cut. Instead, back your V-tool out, flip the project around, and cut back into the dug-in point.

## Tip

The bench knife or the chip carving knife makes excellent V-wedge cuts. I often use the V-tool when the line to be cut runs with the grain of the wood. For cross-grained work, I create cleaner lines with the chip carving knife.

# Texturing the Sides of the Beard

The finishing steps for the mustache and beard include adding small V-shaped cuts along the outer edge of the hair areas. These serrations add interest to the undercut shadows along the beard that we cut earlier.

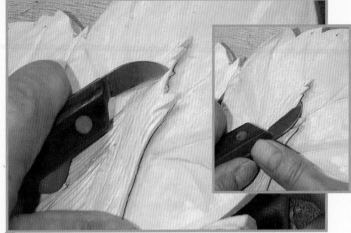

**90** Notice how the edges of the hair areas are fairly smooth. Serrate the edges by adding small V-cuts to imply hair strands. For the first part of this cut, simply push the chip carving knife or the bench knife into the edge section. Make a second cut about ⅟₁₆" to ⅛" away and angled back into the first cut.

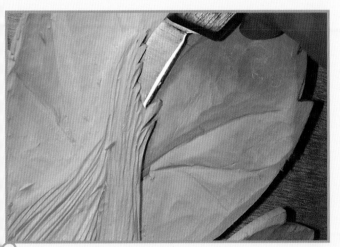

**91** Add variety to the beard by making some cuts small, some large, some deep, and some shallow.

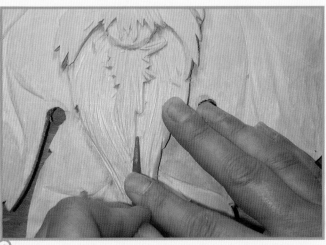

**92** Do a quick cleanup with 220- to 320-grit sandpaper and the riffler along the joint line of the two hair areas and heal any deep stop cuts (see Healing a Cut on page 64). With the completion of this step, the mustache and beard are done.

**93** Do a quick check before you move on to the next section. This photo has only one light source with the light coming in from the upper right side. Notice how the undercutting has forced the beard to stand above the leaf lobes, adding dark shadows inside the project. These inner shadows add to the visual effects of the wall shadows. Also notice the realistic look in the eyes due to the round-gouge cut. The nostrils, also round-gouge cuts, are extremely dark just as they would be on a real face.

# Detailing the Leaves

In this section, we will continue to refine and smooth out the carving. Now, we are headed into the stem and tendril areas of the carving. Because this area has so many ups and downs and grain direction changes, we will be using a variety of tools, including the ⅜" bull-nose chisel, chip carving knife, small and large round gouges, and dogleg chisel.

## The Larger Picture

Our goals for this section:

■ Round over the leaves, stem, and tendrils

■ Add any additional undercuts

■ Clean up any joint lines between elements

■ Smooth any spots that need it on the front and the back

■ Check the shadows using one light source

■ Add serrations to the leaves

# Working the Leaf Tendrils

In this section, the stems and tendrils will be rounded and tucked over or under at the curls. We will also work on cutting into tight, deep areas in the project.

1 Use a pencil to mark the direction of the cuts based on the grain.

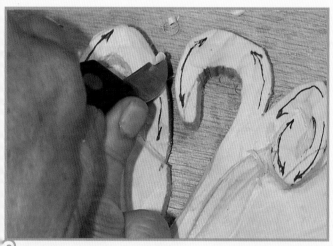

2 Round over the edges with a chip carving knife or a bench knife. Don't worry about the outer side walls at this point. We will catch those when we finish the back of the project. I had to move the project away from the corner of my bracing board, so I am using the side of my right hand to brace the wood with a downward pressure.

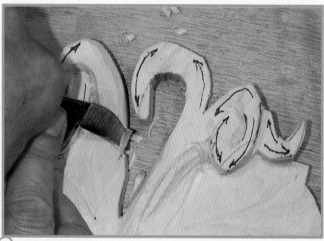

3 Because of the turn or curve of this particular stem, pay attention to the change in the grain direction as you carve. Make cuts from the center of the stem toward the top of the stem to keep the knife running with the grain. In this photo, I had to work my cuts from the center of the stem toward the leaf area to remain with the grain.

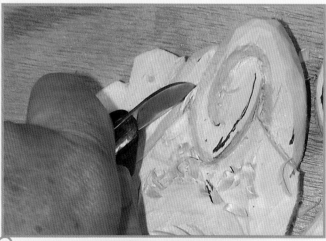

4 Where there are intersections or joints in the stem area, use the chip carving knife to make a small chip cut. This cut cleans out those corner areas.

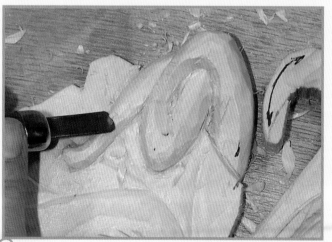

5 Round the center areas of the stem with a ⅜" bull-nose chisel. A straight chisel or a wide-sweep gouge also works well here.

**6** Clean out the space trapped by the twist of the stems with a ⅛" U-gouge.

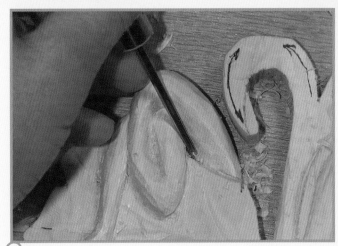

**7** Move into the intersection where the stem goes under the leaf and continue to use the ⅛" U-gouge to trim up and dress out the joint line.

## Tip

I change the size of the round gouge, from a large round to a wide-sweep, depending on the tightness of the area and the curvature of the pattern line.

## Grape Leaves

The grape leaf on the left is a wild grape leaf; the one on the right is domesticated. Notice the wonderful deep cuts that create the five lobes of the domestic grape. That's what we are headed toward. Also notice how textured both leaves are. They have lots of little planes, made from the very fine veins in the leaves, that catch the light. I want that plane look in my carving, so I am not going to sand this piece to remove the chisel- and knife-stroke planes.

# Undercutting the Tendril Curls

A small undercut along the inside edges of the stem visually separates it from the leaf below. Undercutting also allows you to round the bottom area of the stem.

**8** Add an undercut in the curl area. Since the stems are nice and thick, there is ample room to work a deep undercut in this area. This cut will make that part of the stem stand out because of the dark undercut shadow. This cut is the first of two cuts.

**9** Turn the project upside down to make the second cut. You can see how deeply the point is embedded into the undercut area.

**10** Use a dogleg chisel to tease out the wedge of wood created by the undercutting. Any tool that will tuck under this cut to pull out that slice—including the ⅜" straight chisel, the ⁷⁄₃₂" straight chisel, a riffler, or a sandpaper roll—will work here.

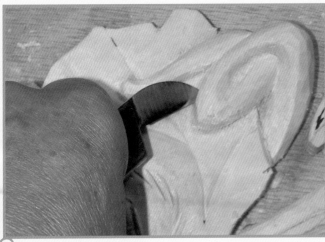

**11** Undercut both sides of the tendril curl so the shadow wraps completely around the curl area.

**12** Remove any wood left in the undercut with the ⅛" U-gouge.

## Tucking Under the Tendril

The next step is to round over and tuck the lower part of the stem under the upper part using a large round gouge for the curve profile.

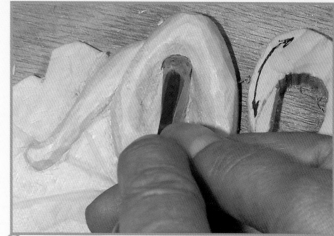

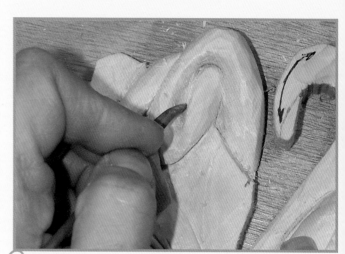

**13** Upend the large round gouge to make a profile cut for the curve of the lower stem. Lay the gouge so its curve is against the curve of the tendril; then, walk or roll the tool back and forth slightly, into the upper stem.

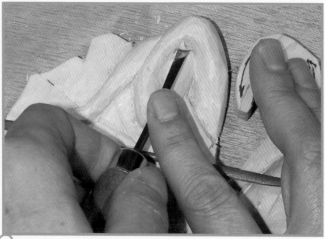

**14** Round the lower stem into the large round gouge's profile cut with the small straight chisel.

**15** Clean up the area with the riffler and the sandpaper roll to finish the inside curl of this tendril.

**16** Cut the second stem curl in the same manner. First, free the small area where the two stems meet with the bench knife or the chip carving knife.

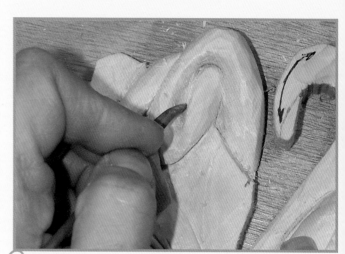

## Tip

Use the profiles of your tools to create shapes in your carving. A small round gouge makes great fish and dragon scales. A V-tool used on profile can make little "V" impressions for background textures. If you need a small, but perfectly straight line, use a straight chisel on its profile.

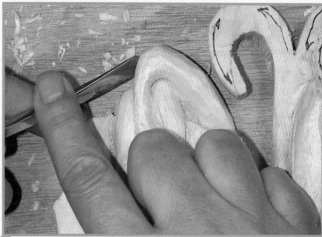

**17** Use the wide-sweep gouge here because the curve is not a tight one. Push gently into the freed intersection to round over the lower stem nicely.

**18** Roll over the tendril side walls with the straight chisel. The straight chisel has a much longer length between the tool's edge and the ferrule area, or metal ring, of the handle than the ⅜" bull-nose chisel. Here, I can get into the side wall easier because of the long tool length.

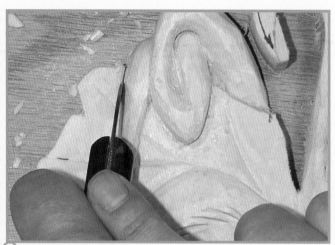

**19** Make a small undercut on the outside edge of the stem. The cut is just big enough to hide the joint line and barely tucks the joint line back underneath the stem.

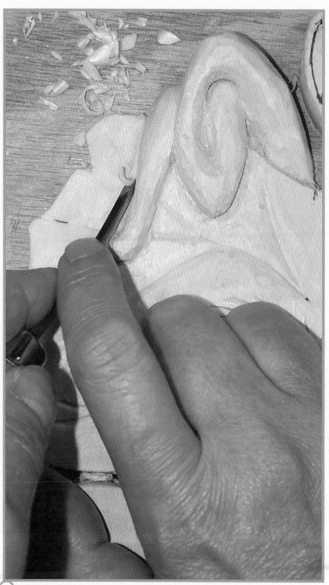

**20** Clean the joint with the ⅜" bull-nose chisel or the ⅜" straight chisel. Not all undercuts in relief carving need to be deep shadow-making cuts. A shallow or small undercut is often used to hide a joint line between two elements.

**21** Use the V-tool to smooth the remaining intersections where the stem and leaf meet. This step includes any area that has not been undercut.

## Rolling a Leaf Edge

The right side of the leaf is carved exactly like the left side that we just completed, with a few exceptions. One exception is that I have lots of room for a very deep undercut on the leaf where it lies on top of the center stem. I will only go over the exceptions for this section.

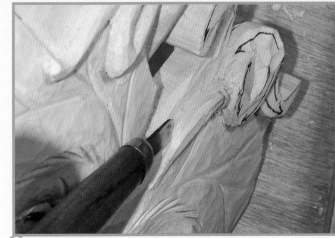

22 The angle of the camera has been adjusted so that you can see into the joint area between the leaf and stem on the right side of the carving. I already have a small angle from the earlier roughing-out work, but I want to really tuck the area.

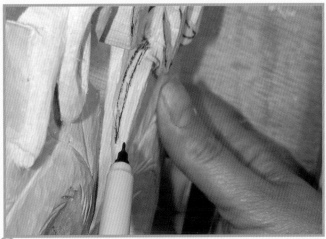

23 Mark the area for the undercut with a pencil. Notice that I have left more than half the thickness above the undercut. I want plenty of room in the wood to roll that top part of the leaf into a nice curve.

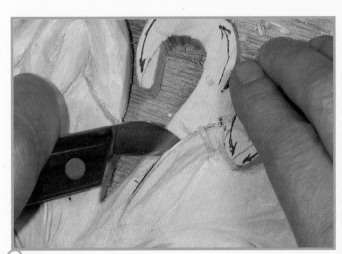

24 Walk the chip carving knife into the depth by making several cuts, not one deep push. This is the deepest undercut on the project.

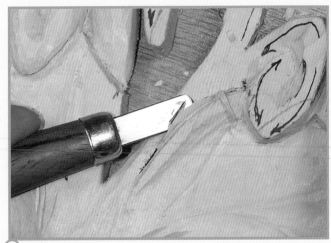

25 Make the second cut of the undercut with the chisel and slice out the wedge in thin pieces. This process takes a little longer but is much easier in hard-to-work places. Roll and round the lower edge of the leaf.

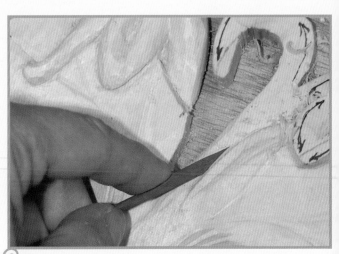

26 Continue making the undercut until you are satisfied with it. Some undercuts, like this one, are deep and very open, exposing the element below the undercut to view. In this area, the stem is revealed. We will detail the area later to add to the realism of the work.

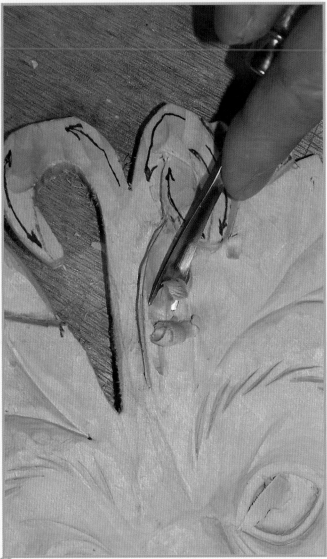

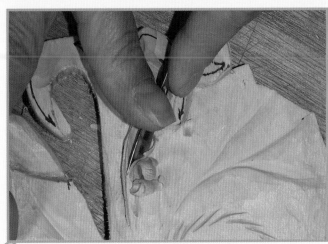

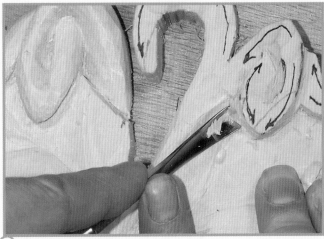

*27* Roll the top of the leaf with the large round gouge or the chisel along the side of the undercut. Don't work directly on the leaf edge. This type of rolling can tear out if it's done too close to the edge. We'll thin the edge later when we add the leaf serrations.

*28* Use the wide-sweep gouge to create a gentle roll on the leaf edge. The size of the gouge determines the tightness of the roll. The large round gouge makes a tighter roll than the wide-sweep gouge; the small round gouge makes a very tight roll or curl in the edge.

*29* Notice how the inside of this rolled leaf edge moves across the grain. Cut the upper section of the roll by working from the center point toward the stem curl.

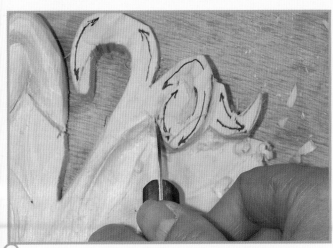

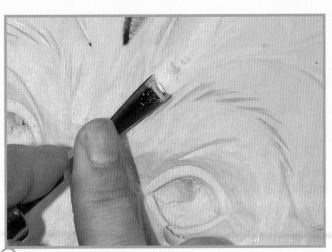

*30* Clean the intersection where the leaf meets the upper stem by making a chip cut.

*31* Recut the brow area with the ⅜" straight chisel, the ⅜" bull-nose chisel, or the wide-sweep gouge, if necessary. The curling of the leaf affects the flow into the brow, so I recut that area. I want a smooth transition from the brow into the leaf and then into the roll over.

## Undercutting the Right-Side Tendril

Now that the stem has been undercut and the leaf edge rolled, the undercut and shaping of the right-side stem can be done.

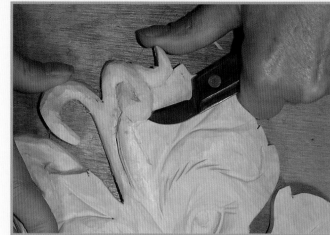

32 Work the stems on the right exactly as those on the left. Here you can see where I am making an undercut. I am using the chip carving knife to create the first stop cut as close to the leaf as possible.

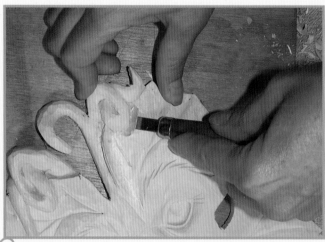

33 Notice how this stem curl was not worked as deeply in the roughing-out stage as the one on the left side. To open the undercut for this side, work from the leaf area and lower the surrounding leaf with long chisel cuts into the undercut.

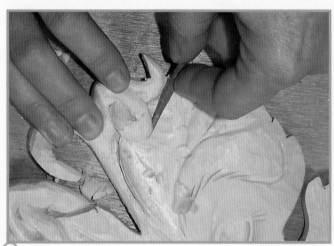

34 Clean up the undercut with chip cuts made with the chip carving knife or bench knife. Then, lightly sand using rolled sandpaper.

35 Smooth the long chisel cuts with the ⅜" bull-nose chisel.

36 Do a quick check. At this point, you should be able to see the twists and turns of the stem. Also note how the leaf has been smoothed into the roll-over edge and how deep the undercut on the right side.

## Smoothing the Back

Because most of the facial sculpturing is completed, it's time to move to the back of the carving to dress out the rough work done earlier. We will refine the shaping along the leaf edges so the flat center area of the project flows smoothly into the rolled areas along the edges.

**37** Clean up and smooth the back of the carving. Start by propping up the piece with white artist's erasers and foam-backed sanding pads. Place the pads sandpaper side down. The sandpaper side grabs the work surface, and the foam side gently supports the wood.

**Tip**

With the facial features, stems, and leaf edges finished for the shaping and smoothing stages, the project no longer sits flat against the bench hook when laid face down. The erasers and sanding pads prevent the work from rocking as you cut the back of the work. If the work rocks, it can cause chips along the front surface or affect your control over the cuts on the back.

**38** Smooth the gouge ridges with the bench knife and the chisel. As I was working, I decided to widen the curved areas so they would cast larger shadows when the piece was displayed.

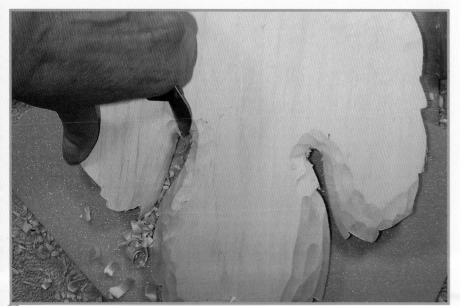

**39** Work the chip carving knife into the tight curve made by the band saw, scroll saw, or coping saw at the beginning cut-out stage. Hold your knife as vertical to the wood as possible to shave the curve smooth.

**Tip**

Wide curves make wide shadows; sharp, short curves make small shadows. You want both wide shadows and small shadows in a relief carving. Don't get carried away and make every curve a wide one. Shadows that flow from thick to thin areas create more interest to your carving than one wide outline of shadowing does.

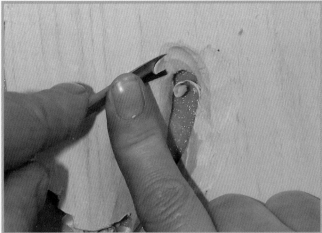

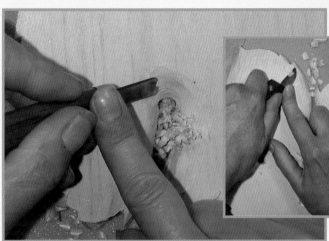

40 Use the large round gouge to taper or smooth out the tight saw curve. I use this tool in a half-circle cut that starts high on the wall of the curve and ends low on the inside of that curve. In the photo, you can see the comma cut just above the gouge tip.

41 Do the final smoothing with the chisel or the wide-sweep gouge. Move along the sides of the back with the chip carving knife. Use Steps 39 and 40—with the chip carving knife widening and the chisel or wide-sweep gouge smoothing—for the long open sections of the sides.

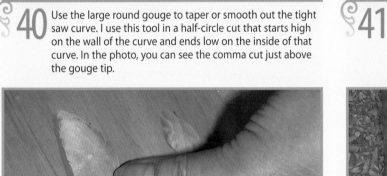

42 Compare the sides before and after the smoothing. I am not going for pristine smooth; remember that the real grape leaf has lots of little planes inside the veins. I want that effect on both the face and the back of this carving.

43 Check the shadows. There is one light source in this photo, coming from the upper right. Look at the wide dark shadow on the lower left side of the bottom leaf lobe where we made the deep cuts. Compare this area to the one above. The second area has little or no rolling on the back at this point.

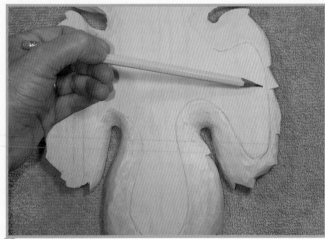

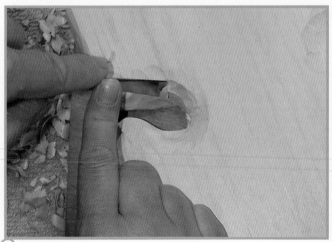

44 If you're not satisfied with the shadows, turn the carving over and rework the back. I marked the inner edge of the back for roll over so you can see how deeply into the back I have worked to create the deep shadow.

45 Continue working on the back with the chip carving knife, large round gouge, chisel, or wide-sweep gouge. You may not be able to reach some places with the work in the bracing board. In these cases, I use a heavy terry cloth towel to hold the wood in my right hand at the angle I need to work comfortably.

## Adding a Leaf Roll from Back to Front

Because there is a lot of thick wood in this area of the back, we have lots of wood to carve a leaf edge that curls over onto the front of the work. These steps will add visual interest to the leaf to match the realistic look of the Grape Man Wood Spirit's face. We will work the two curls on the left side of the project. The lower leaf lobe's edge will curl up and be complemented by the upper leaf lobe's edge curling down.

**46** Locate the area on the back of the carving. The sweep of the gouge will determine the tightness of the leaf curl: Wide-sweep gouges cut open curls and smaller round gouges cut tightly turned curls. Use the ⅜" bull-nose chisel and the chip carving knife to smooth the curl's sides.

**47** Sand the smoothed and tapered edge for both leaf lobes with 220- to 320-grit sandpaper. Sanding will let you see exactly where your working edge is.

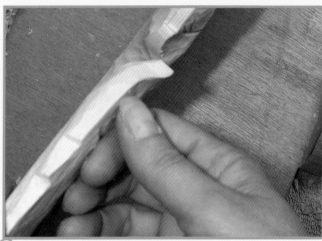

**48** Familiarize yourself with the wood and visualize the results before you begin. As seen from the side or edge view, the top leaf area will be rolled down toward the back to a very thin edge. This will tuck the top leaf under the bottom leaf section. The bottom leaf will roll over onto itself on the face side of the carving.

**49** Begin working on the bottom leaf edge on the face of the carving. Use the large round gouge to create the curl. Notice how far from the edge of the wood I am making that curl. Leave yourself working space away from the edge.

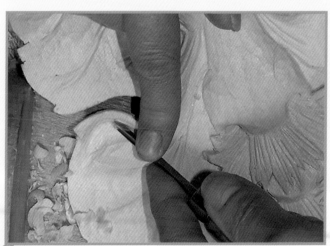

**50** Use the small round gouge and the ⅛" U-gouge to create a sharp, tight curl near the top of the curl area.

$\mathcal{S}$51 Smooth out the two different gouge cuts with the ⅜" bull-nose chisel, blending this area into one curl. The small round gouge will also work. Simply take smaller and smaller shavings with very light pressure until all of the gouge ridges are gone.

$\mathcal{S}$52 Taper the rest of the leaf into the newly curved area. Use either the wide-sweep gouge or the ⅜" bull-nose chisel.

$\mathcal{S}$53 Upend the chisel and use the profile as a scraper to do a final smoothing in this area.

$\mathcal{S}$54 Smooth the side walls of this leaf area with the chip carving knife and tuck it under a little as you work. The leaf should curl on both the front and back of the carving.

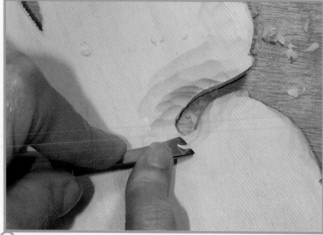

$\mathcal{S}$55 The chip carving knife wasn't big enough to do the job, so I flipped the project over to do the roll over on the back with the wide-sweep gouge. Bigger tools make bigger cuts.

$\mathcal{S}$56 Taper the upper leaf down to a thin edge with the wide-sweep gouge.

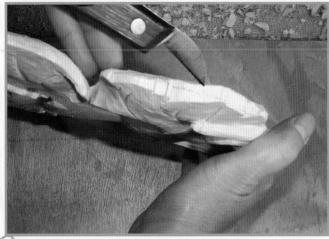

**57** Notice the taper down in the upper leaf from this side view. The upper leaf edge has been cut as deeply as possible, right down to the original back surface of the board. The lower leaf curl rises to the highest point in the original wood.

**58** Recut the upper leaf section with the wide-sweep gouge to make a nice, smooth transition into that deep leaf edge.

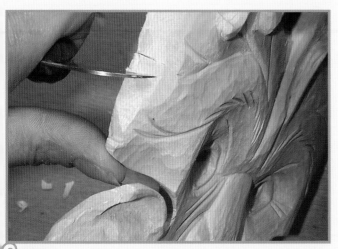

**59** As you work, check for any areas where the band saw, scroll saw, or coping saw cuts were made a little too deep. Take a moment to chip cut them. You can recut this chip as many times as you need to get below the saw cut.

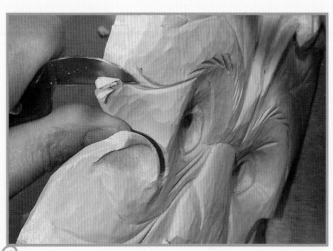

**60** Work along all the sides of the project to do a final tapering and to eliminate any blunt edges. I am also strengthening the V serration in the upper leaf with the chip carving knife.

**61** Do a quick check. All of the edges, the leaf curls and tucks, should be rolled or rounded over so they look paper thin—even though not all of them really are—when viewed from the front of your work.

## Tip

The lower leaf curl becomes more dramatic because of the upper leaf area. Dropping that upper leaf lets your eye compare one very deep area in the carving with one very high area. This side-by-side depth contrast adds to the roll effect of the lower leaf. Your eye would not be as attracted to this lower leaf curl were it not for the dramatic drop of the leaf lobe above it.

## Shaping the Stem

The stem curl is the most fragile area of this carving because the grain direction runs vertically throughout it. We have done very little shaping in this area, so the stem is nearly at the original thickness of the wood. That thickness will help protect the stem during the following steps.

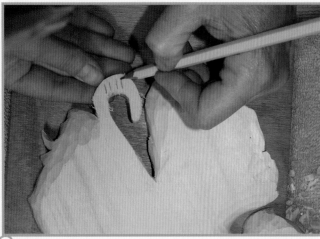

**62** Mark the center section of the stem with a few pencil lines. This area is the most fragile, and the pencil marks give a visual reminder to work this area as little as possible.

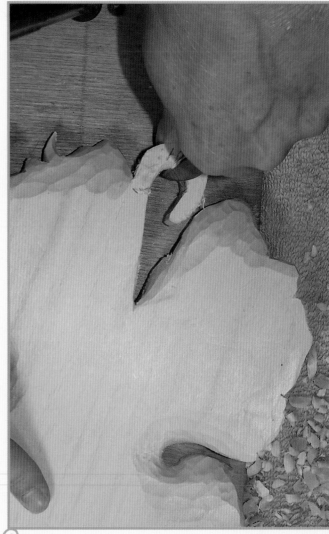

**63** Start with the well-honed chip carving knife, which will not drag or pull on delicate areas of wood. Round over only the edge. At this stage, you don't want to lose any thickness in the height or the width of the stem. I anchor the curve of the stem with my thumb and middle finger to secure this area from rocking due to the cutting strokes.

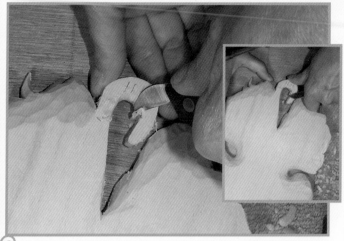

64 If you feel the stem move from the pressure of the knife as you begin working on the second side, set your holding hand, thumb, and finger on the table on both sides of the stem. In this position, your fingers take the pressure of the cut instead of the wood. Here, I am not pressing on the stem but simply bracing the area with my thumb.

65 Start on the outer side of the stem with the chip carving knife, moving your holding hand down to the tip of the stem to catch the cut pressure.

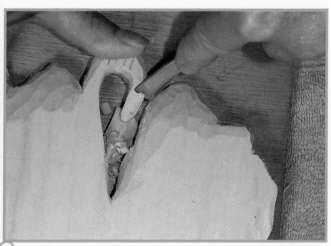

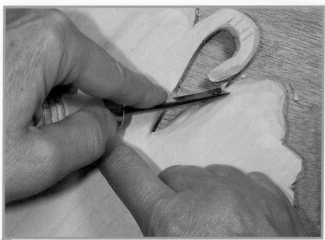

66 Turn the work to the back. Use the chisel or the wide-sweep gouge to taper the tip so that it will be raised away from the wall when the carving is hung. I placed a sliver from an eraser under the stem to catch the pressure of the knife.

67 Round over and taper the stem to finish it. Once the stem has been rolled, continue to secure the area with your noncarving hand, and use a white artist's eraser to remove the pencil marks on the back.

68 The back of the carving is now finished.

69 On the front of the carving, round over the top of the stem tip with the chip carving knife.

## Cutting Serrations on the Leaf Edge

At this point, the leaf has rolls and curls along the leaf edges and deeply cut veins in the center of the lobes. Adding vine serration V-shapes along the outer edge of the leaf lobes will add just a touch of fine detailing to its finished look. Use a variety of depths and lengths in making these serration V-shapes to add interest and contrast.

**70** With a pencil, mark the serrated points along the sides of the leaf to make it into a grape leaf. The two sides of the V-shape serrations are neither straight sided nor equally sized. The top, or upper side, of the V is a short, straight cut into the wood.

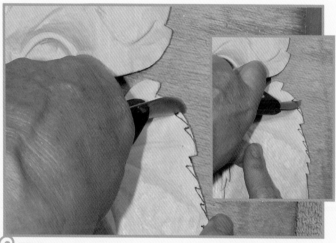

**71** Use the chip carving knife to make the straight cuts that form the serrations. These cuts are similar to the cuts we made to the beard in Step 8 on page 45. For the second cut to the V-shape, roll the chip carving knife cut from the outer leaf edge into the deepest point of the first cut. This will remove the small V-shaped chip.

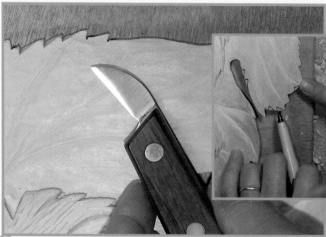

**72** Because leaves do not have perfectly spaced serrations, make a few cuts close together and some far apart. Make some shallow and some deep. Use a pencil to mark the lower portion of this leaf lobe for the serrations so they also point to the center vein of the lobe.

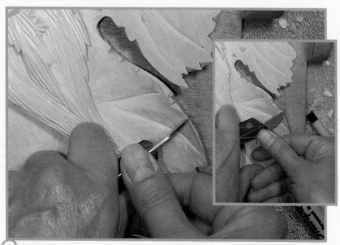

**73** Work the serrations on the rolled-over leaf edge right on the edge. Push the first cut straight into the edge, and then taper the second cut into the first cut.

**74** Go all the way around the outer edge with the serration cuts. The smoothing stage is finished.

# Cleaning Up and Finishing

The last stage to any carving project is the final cleaning steps. In this section, you will be working to remove any loose fibers, smooth out any rough areas, and adjust the rolls or curves in the work.

## The Larger Picture

Our goals for this section:

- Assess the carving and adjust or clean up any areas that need extra attention

- Sand and dust the entire project

- Sign and date the work

- Apply the boiled linseed oil finish and hang the carving

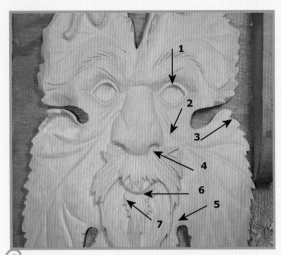

**1** Because I cannot see your project, I cannot tell you exactly where you will need to work during this stage. However, I can show you where my carving needed that little bit of extra work as an example of what you might look for and adjust in your project.

1. Look for double V-tool lines; I have one in the upper eyelid.
2. Recut wobbly V-tool lines. My cheek wrinkle needs to be recut to become one line instead of two V-strokes.
3. Clean up any remaining band saw cutting. I missed a band saw cut along the leaf edge.
4. Check the tapering in the nostril. My mustache has a rough leading edge into the nose.
5. Look for any chip outs along the leaf edge curve; I have a dent in the lower lobe area.
6. Search for any rough edges in the rolled or rounded areas of the face. I need to reshape my lower lip to a better roll.
7. Check the intersections of carving strokes at the corner of the eyes or where one vein joins another for strong angles. I need to recut a double V in that point.

## Cleaning the Surface

Now is the time to clean out those little wood fibers that are still left, crisp up the corners and joints, and check for double V-tool strokes where there should only be one. I call this part of carving "chasing fuzz bunnies." You may want to limit the time you take chasing fuzz bunnies because it can seem that the task is never quite finished. I clean up as many as I can within one evening's worth of work. We'll start with the areas that need the most cleanup and move to more minor cleanup. When we apply oil at the end, you will see that many minor fibers will take care of themselves.

**2** When you have made any fine adjustments as suggested in Step 1, lightly sand the entire project. Use rifflers for the deep undercut areas, foam-core fingernail files for the V-tool cuts, and sandpaper from 220- to 360-grit for the remaining surfaces. Give the carving a good, hard dusting. An old toothbrush in your kit works great for hard-to-reach areas. An air compressor or canned air also works well.

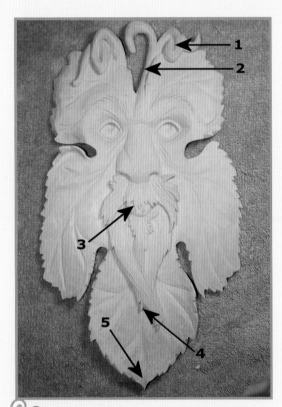

**3** As I was dusting the carving, I found a few more clean-up items that I want to point out.

1. I opened the gap in the stem roll a little more with my veining gouge. I thought the gap in the left side was deeper than the right, so I adjusted the right-side gap.
2. The stem on the face side along the edge of the leaf seemed very square, so I got my chisel and rolled this stem more, both on the face side and the back side.
3. I decided to put a little undercut under the corner of the lip mustache. This adds just a tiny touch of dark shadow at the mouth corners.
4. Because I shaped and veined the leaf lobes before I cut the undercuts beneath the beard, the veins did not go under the beard area. They stopped short! I got my V-tool and carried the veins right underneath and into the undercut area.
5. The center vein stopped short, so I carried this vein down the leaf tip with my V-tool.
6. You might also want to add more Vs to the beard, add more eyebrow hair, or add more V-tool strokes to the beard. The detail in all of these areas can be increased.

# Boiled Linseed Oil Finish

Boiled linseed oil is an easy-to-use finish for our basswood carving. The oil will darken the coloring of the wood and accent the deepest parts of the work. As the carving ages, the linseed oil finish will add a golden tone patina. A great advantage to any oil finish is that you can return to the carving even after the finish is dry and rework areas with additional carving cuts. A spot coating of oil can then be used over those areas. Boiled linseed oil can be used alone as the final coating, or oil or acrylic paints can be applied on top of it to add coloring. Other finishes, such as polyurethane, can be added last as sealers.

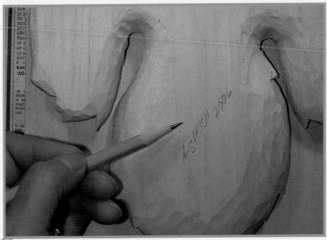

4 Sign and date your work. I sign mine on the back with a pencil. You can also carve your initials or name into this area. Never skip this step!

5 Place clean newspapers on your table, then a scrap board, and then your carving. The scrap board protects your work from any ink in the newspaper. In a pan, mix one part boiled linseed oil with one part turpentine, paint thinner, or mineral spirits. Stir the mix well. Don't shake; you don't want bubbles. Generously brush one coat on the face of the work. You want to flood the work so you have some puddles.

6 When the carving is swimming in oil, go back and continue to brush over the carving. Move the heavy puddles out into areas where the oil is disappearing quickly. Wipe everything with a clean, lint-free cotton cloth to remove the excess. Set the carving aside for an hour or two. When the first coat is dry, turn the piece over to do the back.

7 Work through these steps to apply a second coat of oil. Then, let the carving sit until tomorrow. The completed project is ready to display.

## Tip

Remember to dispose of any oily rags properly. When you are finished with the oil in each step, take your newspaper and rags outside. These are very flammable. I soak the rags and paper in soapy water when I am completely done to break down the oil.

# Part 3

# Patterns

Once you have successfully carved the Grape Man Wood Spirit, give some of these patterns a try. All of them are designed to use and build upon the techniques you learned through carving the demonstration project.

# Classic Woodspirit

# Long Maple Leaf Panel

# Maple Leaf One

Instructions for the
maple backboard appear
on pages 125-127.

# Maple Leaf Two

# Maple Leaf Three

# North Wind Wood Spirit

# Tall Celtic Twist

# Leaves

# Tutorial 1: Dry Brush Painting Your Wood Spirit

The completed painted wood spirit project.

This fun wood spirit—Woodie— is a relief carving worked deeply into four-quarter (1") basswood. Basswood is wonderful for detailed carvings because of its soft tight grain but it has little or no color characteristics to enhance the finished work. Unlike walnut or butternut, basswood tends to be a very flat off-white color throughout the wood. So we will be working on a simple, easy, and fun technique to create a colorful wood-grained effect using acrylic paints as a base coat and oil paints as a staining coat. After achieving the wood grain effect, we will add a small amount of coloring for the face and dry brush the hair. Because this is a tutorial on the painting steps, we will just look at a brief overview of the carving stages. This wood spirit carving followed the same basic steps as the carving of the Grape Man.

Begin by tracing your pattern to the basswood blank. Using a band saw or scroll saw, cut the basswood along the wood spirit outline. You do not need to cut every little V shape along the hairlines.

Cut only the larger V's. The small ones can be cut during the carving stage with your V-gouge. After cutting, break the design down into levels for easy rough out work.

Next, follow through the steps in carving the Grape Man to create this wonderful little wood spirit. Finish with light sanding, if needed, using 220-grit sandpaper or higher.

## Base Coats

After completing your carving, remove any remaining chips, fibers, or dust with a stiff brush and lint-free cloth.

Step one is to create a colorful base coating to the wood spirit using acrylic paints. On your palette, mix approximately three parts titanium white with one part raw sienna. You want a mixture close to the original basswood color. You can add just a couple of drops of water to the mix to thin it slightly. This will help ensure the color easily fills the deep V-gouge cuts and tight joint lines.

Using a large ox-hair brush, scrub one coat of the mix to the entire work. Allow it to dry well,

## Carving Supplies:

Four-quarter basswood
Band saw or scroll saw
Straight chisel
Round gouge
V-gouge and skew
Bench knife or chip carving knife
Sharpening stones

## Artist Supplies Needed:

**Acrylic Artist Paints**
  Titanium white
  Raw sienna
  Burnt umber

**Oil Artist Paints**
  Burnt umber
  Raw sienna
  Cadmium yellow medium
  Cadmium red
  Polyurethane spray sealer

Linseed oil
Turpentine
Large ox-hair brush for the base coating of acrylics
Large soft-staining brush for the oil stain
Assorted small soft brushes for dry brushing
Soft lint-free cloths
Water pans, mixing pans
Paint palette
Lint-free cloths
Paper towels

about one-half hour. You can use a hair dryer to quicken the drying time.

When the first coat is well dried, apply a second coat of the base mix. I like to turn a work upside down for the second coating. This lets me get color into areas the first coat may have missed. Once the second coat is applied, allow it to dry well.

The streaking steps you will be doing next involve working wet paint on wet paint. Do not wait for each streaking color to dry before adding the next and blend the streaking strokes into new shades of color.

To the remaining base coat mixture, add an equal part of raw sienna. Load your large ox-hair brush with the new mixture, and blot off any excess color from the brush. Working vertically, pull several streaks of the mix across the work. Place the streaks randomly.

Repeat the streaking step using unmixed raw sienna. Mix a small amount of burnt umber to the raw sienna and add a few more streaks. For final streaking, use titanium white.

Allow the streak coating to dry well. Your carving should be colorful at this point, with changing streaks of color throughout the work.

The base coat is streaked with several different shades of brown acrylic to create the impression of wood grain. Work the wet streaks to create new color shades.

## Stain Coats

When your base coats of acrylic have dried well, apply several light coats of polyurethane spray sealer to the entire work. Let each coat dry well before applying the next. Follow the directions on the spray can.

In a small pan, mix one part burnt umber oil paint with one-half part linseed oil. The oil paint-linseed mixture should be thin, but not runny. Using a large soft-staining brush, apply one coat of the mix over your work. Work the oil stain into the deep crevices.

After covering the work with oil stain, wipe the piece using a lint-free cloth. As you wipe, the stain will saturate your cloth. As it does, refold the lint-free cloth so you are using a clean area. Remove the excess oil stain. Your work should have a light to medium brown look on the high areas with heavy staining in deep crevices.

You can spot-stain large carvings for more control over coloring. Apply the oil stain in small sections, approximately 3" or 4" square. Wipe the area with the lint-free cloth, then repeat those two steps for the next area.

Slightly moisten a clean cloth with turpentine. Wrap the cloth around one finger for support and lightly rub it over the high areas of the carving to pick up the burnt umber oil stain from just the highest ridges of your work. Allow the oil stain to dry well, usually overnight.

Your carving should have a wood grain look with changing color tones with the base color of the wood and dark umber tones in the deepest crevices.

A mixture of burnt umber and linseed oil has been used to stain the work. Notice how the mix darkens deep crevices of the carving. The impression of wood graining created by acrylic streaking shows through the oil stain.

## Dry Brush and Roughing

When your oil staining has dried well, apply several light coats of polyurethane spray sealer to the entire work. Let each coat dry well before applying the next. Follow the directions on the spray can.

For the face coloring, place a small amount of raw sienna oil paint on a palette. Add a drop or two of linseed oil until the paint is thin, but not running. Wrap a clean lint-free cloth around your finger and pat the cloth into the raw sienna-linseed oil mix. On a paper towel, pat most of the color off the cloth. Using a circular motion, rub the cloth over the skin area of your carving. A very fine coating of raw sienna will adhere to the work. You can apply several coats. Two or three coats will create a nice medium skin color.

Mix a small amount of cadmium yellow medium and cadmium red oil paints to create an orange tone. Working the skin area, pick some color up on a cloth-wrapped finger, blot, then apply the color to the cheek areas and tip of the nose. One coat will probably be enough. Add a second for a stronger blush.

Rubbing thin layers of oil paint over a stained work is called roughing. This is a great technique to use for color buildup because the color sits on top of the stain, not under it, keeping the color bright. If you need more than a few layers of color, add a layer of polyurethane spray between coats.

The hair has been dry brushed with acrylic paints. Place a small amount of titanium white on your palette. Moisten a small soft-shade brush with water then blot the brush on a paper towel. Pick up a small amount of titanium white on your brush tip. On a clean area of the palette, work the white into the brush by pulling it back and forth across the palette several times. Pull the brush across the hair area. You are working against the carved texture grain. As you pull the brush, a small amount of white will be left on the high ridges of the texture but no white will reach the deep brown crevices. Apply one light coat of dry brushed white to all of the hair sections.

Pick a few sections of hair that you want brighter than the rest. Dry brush a second coat of white just to these areas. I chose the mustache, eyebrows, temple hair, and his bangs. Add a third coat to just a few places and along the edges of the hair clumps. My third coats went on the eyebrows, bangs, temple hair, and on the edges of his mustache.

Of note here, I carved out the pupil of the eyes using a round gouge. At this stage, that area should be very darkly colored from the oil staining steps. On the round areas of the eye, apply one thin coat of titanium white. Add a small amount of burnt umber to the titanium white to create a medium-brown tone. Load a soft square shade brush with the mix and blot most of the color from the brush on a paper towel. Use the lightly loaded brush to pull a shadow on the round area of the eye under the upper eyelid. This shades the eye giving it a more natural look than just plain white eyes.

Allow the acrylic dry brushing to dry well. Give your work a final coating of polyurethane spray.

You can add color to a work that has already been stained and set with polyurethane sealer by roughing oil colors. Thin layers of oil paint can be rubbed over the stained area using several coats to develop the color intensity. Dry brushing with acrylics is a great technique for highlighting deeply textured areas as hair. Drag a lightly loaded brush across the grain and the color will only grab the high areas of the carving.

# Tutorial 2: Three Oaks Close Up

Throughout the Grape Man instructions, we have worked on a wood spirit with a face that has a full frontal view, but some wood spirit patterns will have partial frontal views or profile views. The Long Oaks design shows three leaf spirits each slightly turned away from a full frontal position. Let's look at a few of the techniques that make the faces turn to one side or the other.

Start by comparing two faces, the Long Oak pattern to the Woodie wood spirit pattern.

Long Oak pattern (left) and Woodie closeup.

The completed Three Oaks project.

Woodie is a full frontal view. Each area of the face is a mirror image of the opposite side. The nose walls are straight and even with the wall on the left side of the nose the same as the wall on the right side. The upper eyelids and the brow ridge are carved straight into the board with no slanting or sloping. The nostrils are the same size and shape with no undercutting and the eyes have the same mirror image shape. The shadows throughout the Woodie carving are also even and mirrored on each side.

The Long Oak face turns slightly and his face is not a mirror image face. Most notable is the facial features are not laid out with straight or parallel lines. Instead, the left side of the face is not as tall as the right side. Turn your head for a moment to your left and look down toward the floor. In this position, you can feel your jaw and cheek areas compress against your shoulder. You can feel your cheek areas wrinkle to compensate for the pressure of your cheek against your shoulder. The compression makes the left side of your face slightly shorter then the right side. That is the same compressed position our leaf spirit has in this pattern.

Because of the slight twist to his face, you can see more of one side of his nose then the other.

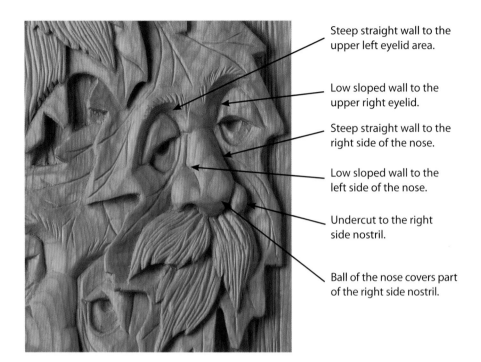

Steep straight wall to the upper left eyelid area.

Low sloped wall to the upper right eyelid.

Steep straight wall to the right side of the nose.

Low sloped wall to the left side of the nose.

Undercut to the right side nostril.

Ball of the nose covers part of the right side nostril.

The full nose side has a long gentle slope to the centerline of the nose. The far side of the nose wall drops into a thin steep slope away from the center area. The ball of the nose is well away from the left nostril but covers part of the right nostril making that one appear smaller. To accentuate the turn of the nose, I have added an undercut along the lower right nose wall and right nostril. You can see the long dark shadow down the entire right side of the nose.

The second major change of a turned face is in the upper eyelid areas. Notice how the right side of the face has a wider, more exposed upper eyelid then the left side. Because of the twist to his left of the entire face, that right side upper eyelid becomes more exposed where the left side upper eyelid becomes compressed. The left upper lid takes on a steep sharp angle into the eye area.

The two sides of the upper eyelids into the nose wall areas of the Oak Leaf's face have been highlighted for comparison. You can see on the left that the upper eyelid starts tight, with steep walls, then flows down into the broad low sloping walls of the nose. On the right side, the upper lid area is the open, low sloping portion of the facial curve that flows into the tight, steep slope of the right nose wall. By changing the slopes and angles of the two sides of the face, you turn the face away from a full front view.

# Tutorial 3: Adding Extra Depth

This fun little wood spirit—"George"—was created to be a hat rack for my husband's favorite baseball cap. George is worked from three pieces of basswood—one for the back support board, one for his face, and one for his nose, mustache and lip beard. By using several layers of basswood, George has added depth to his face when the carving is completed.

When I laid the design out of the basswood blanks, I traced the pattern for the back support first, and then did a complete tracing for his face. Next, I made another tracing of just his nose, mustache, and lip beard areas. The three tracings were cut with the band saw. After a good sanding of the band saw-cut edges along the nosepiece, I used wood glue to secure the nose to the face. The two pieces were securely clamped and set aside until the next day to allow the wood glue to dry well.

To provide the area needed for the baseball cap to go over his head, I have used dowel pins to support the wood spirit on the backboard. The pins are long enough to easily grab into both pieces of wood, yet allow about ½" of air space between them for the back of the hat.

Once the backboard was cut on the band saw, I made three pencil marks for my dowel pins. The backboard was clamped on top of a scrap board, just as we did in Step 5 (page 40), and I drilled the holes all the way through the backboard using a drill bit the same width as my dowel pins. The large knothole was drilled next using a ¾" Forstner bit and the small knot was done with a ⅜" Forstner bit.

The early stages of carving: notice how the added nosepiece will give the final carving extra depth. Once the glue has dried well and you begin your carving cuts you will work the nose area as if it were the highest layers of your carving.

Three pieces combine into one finished work.

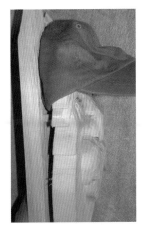

New uses for a mounted wood spirit carving.

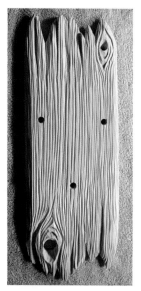

the linseed oil, apply one generous coating of the oil exactly as we worked with the Grape Leaf Spirit. Wipe the excess oil with a clean cloth. If you are pleased with the color toning, apply your second coat of oil using just linseed oil. If you want your backboard darker in color, use the burnt umber/linseed oil mix for your second coat. The wood spirit was finished using uncolored boiled linseed oil.

After the backboard tracing was cut on the band saw, I placed the wood spirit face blank into position on the backboard. Next, I used a pencil to mark on the backboard exactly where the face would lie.

With the dowel pins dry-set into place, you can transfer the dowel pin placement to the back of the wood spirit face. Drill the holes in the back of the face only ¼" deep.

I created the wood grain effect using my bench knife to create wide stop cuts for the heavy grain areas and my V-gouge for lighter or shallow grain. I used my large round gouge to angle the two Forstner bit holes to add more interest to these knotholes.

After the carvings are complete, the dowel pins are glued into place into the backboard and the wood spirit. By placing several pieces of ½" scrap wood between the backboard and the wood spirit during the gluing steps, you can create the air space needed for the baseball cap placement.

To add color to the backboard, I added a small amount of burnt umber artist oil paint to my boiled linseed oil. Approximately ¼" of oil paint was added to ⅓ cup of linseed oil. Mix well. Once the burnt umber is well distributed throughout

Finishing your wood spirit hat rack.

The instructions for the Maple backboard shown at left would be the same as for George's backboard (below right). It is just a different backboard to choose for your design. The idea of George was that any of the green men and wood spirits can be mounted.

Patterns appear at 60% of actual size.

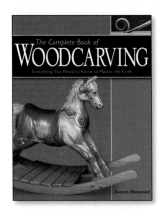
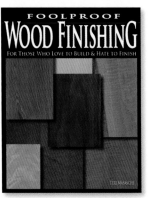